DON'T SWEAT
THE SMALL STUFF
WITH YOUR FAMILY

DON'T SWEAT THE SMALL STUFF WITH YOUR FAMILY

Simple Ways to Keep Daily Responsibilities

and Household Chaos from

Taking Over Your Life

RICHARD CARLSON, PH.D.

New York

DESIGNED BY JENNIFER ANN DADDIO

FIRST EDITION

10 9 8 7 6 5 4 3 2 1

I dedicate this book to my family—
Kris, Jazzy, and Kenna. I am so blessed
to share my life with you. Thank you for
being just the way you are and for
forgiving me when I sweat the
small stuff with you!

ACKNOWLEDGMENTS

I would like to express my most sincere gratitude to my family and friends for providing me with helpful material and great solutions in learning to not sweat the small stuff! Most particularly, I'd like to thank my wife, Kris, for her tremendous support and assistance in creating this book. Not only did she come up with many of the ideas, but she is also excellent in putting them into practice. I'd also like to thank Leslie Wells, clearly one of the finest editors in publishing, as well as Patti Brietman and Linda Michaels, for your never-ending support, skill, and encouragement. I love working with all of you. Finally, I'd like to thank all my friends at Hyperion, especially Vicky Chew, Jennifer Landers, and Jennifer Lang for the tremendous contributions you have made in my behalf.

CONTENTS

DON'T SWEAT
THE SMALL STUFF
WITH YOUR FAMILY

INTRODUCTION

Whether it's with your kids, your spouse, parents, a relative, a teenager, a sibling, or some combination of the above, chances are "family dynamics" are, at times, a little difficult. The familiarity, inevitable habits, expectations, sacrifice, conflicting agendas, quirks, responsibility, and all sorts of other "family stuff" can contribute to a stressful environment. Plus, family members, perhaps more than almost anyone else, really know how to push our buttons! Add to the family dynamics all the responsibilities and annoyances around the home—bills, dishes, cleaning, expenses, piles of clutter, thin walls, yard work, phone calls, pets, neighbors, laundry, noise, upkeep, and so forth—and you've got yourself the makings of a nervous breakdown. Let's be honest. Being part of a family is a privilege and certainly rewarding, but it can also be a little difficult, even when things are going well. If you want to have an effective, loving experience of family, you must learn to be patient and to not let the little things drive you crazy and take over your life. There are certainly enough difficult things to deal with regarding family and home life. So, the truth is, if you sweat the small stuff at home, you're probably setting yourself up to be a nervous wreck. To me, this is a very important topic to cover. The stakes are high—the harmony in your home, even your own sanity.

I have written this book to help make life with family and around the home a little easier and, hopefully, more loving. The strategies are designed to address some of the most common sources of frustration and to help bring back the joy of home life that can sometimes get lost in the minor frustrations and busyness of daily living. The strategies are designed to heighten your perspective, patience, and wisdom. They will help you respond to your family and home life more gracefully and with more gratitude and ease.

People who learn to not sweat the small stuff with family and around the home have an enormous edge in life. They expend far less energy being irritated and frustrated and have more left over for having fun and being productive and loving. The energy that used to be spent being "stressed out" is now focused on creativity and the creation of joyful experiences and memories. When little things don't get to you so much, your family will seem more like a source of joy than ever before. You'll be more patient and easygoing. Your life will seem easier. You will feel less burdened and hassled, and you'll experience more harmony in your life. This peaceful feeling will spread and will be experienced by the others in your family.

When you learn to keep things in perspective and become less easily bothered, your days will seem easier and far less stressful. You'll see the innocence in other people and in some of the behaviors that used to drive you crazy. This will make you feel closer as a family unit and more peaceful as an individual. Thus, you'll be easier on yourself and less attached to having to have things a certain way in order for you to be happy. You'll have more love in your heart and will share that love with those around you. Finally, you'll become less reactive, which will help you bring out the best in those you love most.

Having written *Don't Sweat the Small Stuff,* many people have asked me, "Is it always peaceful around *your* home?" I must confess that it is not! From the moment *Don't Sweat the Small Stuff* hit the bookstores, my kids, in particular, have held me to a higher standard than ever before. Now, it seems like I can't get away with anything. For example, on more than one occasion when I've managed to get too uptight or reactive about something at home, my youngest daughter, Kenna, has run around the house holding a copy of the book and yelling, "Don't sweat the small stuff, Daddy. Don't sweat the small stuff!" My eight-year-old daughter, Jazzy, is even tougher on me than her sister. Recently, she and I were having breakfast on a day I was flying across the country to help teach a corporation to be a little more relaxed and stress-free. While we were eating and having a "heart-to-heart" conversation, I somehow shifted the conversation and started to lecture her—something she absolutely can't stand. At some point she stood up. She then put her hands on her hips and said, in a loving but sarcastic tone, "Come on, Dad, do you *really* teach people to relax?" Indeed, I admit it. I sweat the small stuff more with my family than anywhere else. And I'll bet you do, too!

None of us is ever going to bat 100 percent, or even close to it, when dealing with our own family and home life. There will always be times when we will feel frustrated or overwhelmed. However, we can make a significant dent. We can make incremental, sometimes even drastic, improvements in the way we relate to those in our family and to the responsibilities of daily living. Indeed, we can significantly improve the quality of our lives as individuals and as a family.

The desire to "not sweat the small stuff" has become a priority in the lives of millions of people. Nowhere is this more important than around those we love. As we become a little more relaxed and calm, we will avoid the common tendency to take our family and loved ones for granted. Instead, we will appreciate the gift of family and, indeed, the gift of life. As you incorporate these ideas into your life you will begin to create a more peaceful and loving family. I send you and your family my love and best wishes.

1.

SET A POSITIVE EMOTIONAL CLIMATE

Just like a garden that flourishes best under certain conditions, your home operates more smoothly when the emotional climate is well thought out. Rather than simply reacting to each crisis and circumstance as it arises, setting an emotional climate gives you a head start to fending off potential sources of stress and conflict. It helps you respond to life rather than react to it.

When trying to determine the ideal emotional environment for yourself and/or your family, there are several important questions to ask yourself: What type of person are you? What type of environment do you enjoy and thrive in? Do you wish your home were more peaceful? These types of questions are critical in order to set the optimal emotional climate.

The creation of an emotional climate has more to do with your inner preferences than your external environment. For example, the placement of your furniture or the colors of your walls or carpet can contribute to the emotional environment but are not the most critical ingredients. Your emotional environment is primarily made up of things like noise levels, the speed of activity (is everyone rushing around like a chicken with its head cut off?), the respect of one another, and the willingness (or lack of willingness) to sit still and listen.

In our home, for example, we have determined that our goal is to create and maintain an environment of relative calm. Although we often fall short of our goal, we do take steps to put the odds in our favor. For example, although we all love spending time together, and we very often do, each of us also enjoys spending time alone in our home. The simple recognition that being alone is thought of as positive, rather than as negative, makes it easier for all of us to be sensitive to the noise, activity, and chaos levels that are occurring at any given moment. We have learned to sense when one of us needs a quieter environment or the space to be alone.

Another thing we try to do is to keep unnecessary rushing around to a minimum. Even though our children are only eight and five years old, we have discussed this issue many times. As a family, we have agreed to work on this tendency as individuals as well as in our interactions together. For example, if I fall into my habit of rushing around, trying to do too many things at once, I've given my children permission to gently remind me to slow down. They know that keeping a sane pace is important to the quality of our life at home and they feel comfortable reminding me when I'm interfering with this goal.

Obviously, the ideal emotional environment is going to be different from home to home. However, I think you'll find that if you spend a little time reflecting on what type of environment you would most prefer, you'll see relatively simple changes that you can begin to implement. Be patient with this one. It may have taken many years to create your current emotional environment, so it may take a little time to create a new one. Over time, I'm fairly certain you'll find this strategy extremely rewarding.

2.

GIVE YOURSELF AN EXTRA

TEN MINUTES

When you ask a typical person or family about what stresses them out the most, it's rare that someone doesn't include the fact that they are almost always running "a few minutes behind." Whether you're off to a soccer match, work, the airport, a neighborhood picnic, a typical day at school, or church, it seems that most of us almost always find a way to wait until the last possible minute to leave, thus running a little late. This tendency creates a great deal of unnecessary stress as we're constantly thinking about who is waiting for us, how far we are behind schedule, and how often this occurs. Invariably, we end up clutching the steering wheel, tightening our neck, and worrying about the consequences of being late. Running late makes us feel stressed out and encourages us to sweat the small stuff!

This ever-so-common problem is easily solved by simply giving yourself an extra ten minutes to get yourself and your family to your appointments. Irrespective of where you're headed, tell yourself that, no matter what, you're going to be ten minutes *early* instead of waiting until the last possible moment to rush out the door.

The key, of course, is to start getting ready a little earlier than usual and to be sure you're all-the-way ready before you start doing something else. I can't tell you how much this simple strategy has helped me in my own life. Rather than constantly scrambling to find my daughters' shoes or my wallet at the last possible moment, I'm now usually ready with plenty of time to spare. Don't kid yourself that these extra ten minutes aren't significant—they are. The extra few minutes before and between activities can be the difference between a stressful day and a joyful day. In addition, you'll discover that when you're not running late you'll be able to enjoy rather than rush through the different things you do each day. Even simple, ordinary events can be great fun when you're not in such a hurry.

When you're done with one activity, leave a little earlier for the next one. When possible, try to schedule your activities, work, play, and everything else a little further apart. Finally, don't overschedule. Allow for some downtime, time where absolutely nothing is scheduled.

If you implement this strategy, you'll be amazed at how much more relaxed your life will seem. The constant sense of pressure, of rushing around, scrambling, will be replaced with a quiet sense of peace.

3.

KEEP IN MIND THAT A HAPPY SPOUSE
IS A HELPING SPOUSE

This is such an obvious concept that I'm almost embarrassed to write about it. Yet, I've found that very few marriages take advantage of the truly remarkable ramifications of this strategy. The idea, of course, is that when your spouse is happy and feels appreciated, he or she will want to be of help to you! On the other hand, when your spouse feels unhappy and/or taken for granted, the last thing in the world he or she will feel like doing is making *your* life easier!

Let me make it perfectly clear that I'm not suggesting that it's your responsibility to make your spouse happy. It's ultimately up to each person to make that happen for himself or herself. We do, however, play a significant role in whether or not our spouses feel appreciated. Think about your own situation for a moment. How often do you *genuinely* thank your spouse for all the hard work he or she does on your behalf? I've met hundreds of people who admit to virtually never thanking their spouses in this way, and almost no one who does so on a regular basis.

Your spouse is your partner. Ideally, you'd treat your partner as you would your best friend. If your best friend, for example, said to you, "I would love to get away by myself for a few days," what would you say? In most cases, you'd probably come back with something like, "That sounds great. You deserve it. You should do it." But if your *spouse* said exactly the same thing, would your reaction be the same? Or would you think about how his or her request would affect you? Would you feel put out, defensive, or resentful? Is a good friend more concerned with himself or herself, or with the happiness of the other person? Do you think it's a coincidence that your good friends love to help you whenever possible?

Obviously, you can't always treat your spouse in exactly the same way you would your other good friends. After all, running a marriage and/or a household as well as a joint budget carries with it a great deal of responsibility. However, the dynamic can be similar. For example, if a good friend came over and cleaned your house and then took the time to make your dinner, what would you say? How would you react? If your spouse does the very same thing, doesn't he or she deserve the same recognition and gratitude? Most certainly. Whether our jobs involve staying at home, working out of the house, or some combination of the two, we all love and deserve to be appreciated. And when we don't feel taken for granted, our natural instinct is to be of help.

Almost nothing is more predictable than the way people respond when they feel appreciated and valued. Both my wife and I genuinely appreciate each other and try to remember to never take each other for granted. I love it when Kris tells me how much she appreciates all my hard work, and she continues to let me know, even after more than thirteen years of marriage. I also try to remember to acknowledge and express my gratitude daily for her hard work and for her enormous contribution to our family. The result is that we both love to do things for each other—not just out of obligation but because we know that we are appreciated.

You may be doing the same thing already. If so, keep it up. But if not, it's never too late to start. Ask yourself, What could I do to express my gratitude toward my spouse even more than I already do? Usually, the answer is very simple. Make an ongoing effort to say "Thank you," and do so genuinely. Keep in mind not so much what you are doing for the relationship, but what your spouse is doing. Express your gratitude and appreciation. I bet you'll notice what all happy couples do—that the happier and more appreciated your spouse feels, the more often he or she will reach out to help you.

4.

LEARN FROM KIDS AS THEY
LIVE IN THE MOMENT

This strategy is workable whether or not you have children living at home, or even if you've never had kids of your own. You can spend time around other people's children, or simply observe them at a local park. While it's certainly not always true, for the most part children naturally live in the moment. This is especially true for younger kids.

To experience life in the "present moment" is not a mysterious endeavor, nor is it any big deal. Essentially, all it involves is putting less attention on worries, concerns, regrets, mistakes, "what's wrong," things yet to be done, things that bother you, the future, and the past. Living in the present simply means living life now, with your attention fully engaged in this present moment, not allowing your mind to carry you away to experiences removed from this moment. When you manage to do this, you not only enjoy the moment you are experiencing to the fullest extent possible, you also bring out the best in your performance and creativity because you are far less distracted by your wants, needs, and concerns.

Happy people know that regardless of what happened yesterday, last month, years ago—or what might happen later today, tomorrow, or next year—now is the only place where happiness can actually be found and experienced. Obviously, this doesn't mean you aren't affected by, or that you don't learn from, your past—or that you don't plan for tomorrow (or for retirement and so forth), only that you understand that your most effective, powerful, and positive energy is the energy of today—the energy of right now. When you're bothered or upset, it's usually over something that is over or something else that is yet to be.

Children intuitively understand that life is a series of present moments, each meant to be experienced wholly, one right after another, as if each one is important. They immerse themselves in the present and offer their full attention to the person they are with. I remember an endearing incident that occurred five or six years ago. My wife and I had hired a baby-sitter to watch our then-two-year-old while we went out for the evening. My daughter and I were playing in her sandbox, having a great time together, when the sitter arrived. As I stood to leave, my daughter let out a fierce scream of disapproval. It was as if she were saying, "How dare you interrupt our fun together!" She yelled and screamed and complained that she didn't want the sitter—it *had* to be me. But, shortly after we "escaped," I realized that I had forgotten my car keys and I went inside to get them. I peeked out the back door and saw that my daughter was all smiles and laughter, playing, once again, in the sandbox. She was absorbed in her beautiful present moments. She had completely let go of the past—even though the past was only a few minutes old.

How often does an adult effectively do that? A psychologist or cynic might say she was being manipulative toward me—and there may be a grain of truth in that assumption. However, a happy person would recognize that she was simply voicing her strong objection in one moment and then moving on to the next. Once I had left the scene, she freely returned her focus to the here and now—an excellent lesson for us all.

As you take this strategy to heart, you will discover that being able to immerse yourself in the present moment is a worthwhile quality to strive for. Doing so gives you the capacity to experience ordinary events in an extraordinary fashion. You will spend far less time being bothered by life, while spending more time enjoying it. You'll spend less energy convincing yourself that right now isn't good enough and more time enjoying the special moment you are in—this one.

5.

PROTECT YOUR PRIVACY

Your home is your haven, an escape from the outside world. When you allow too much of the craziness from the outside to enter your home, you eliminate, or at least reduce, a potential source of peace. While most of us are concerned with protecting our physical safety, and will take steps to secure it, we often forget or even neglect our emotional and spiritual "safety." We can do this, at least in part, by honoring our need for some degree of privacy.

Protecting and respecting your own privacy is a statement to yourself and others that you value yourself and your own peace of mind. It suggests that your sanity and happiness are extremely important. Your home is one of the few places where, in most instances, you have some degree of control over what enters and what doesn't. Home is often a place where you have the power to say no.

Protecting your privacy can involve many things. It might mean letting your answering machine pick up your messages or screen your calls so that you don't have to. Often, out of pure habit, we rush to pick up the phone when we really don't want to talk to anyone. Is it any wonder we feel overwhelmed or crowded? I have a general policy that I won't answer the phone when I feel like being alone or when

I'm already with someone in my family who wants or needs my attention. Why is it that we interrupt the ones we love to answer a call from someone we may not even know?

If you have children, you might try putting a cap on the number of friends you invite to come over in any given week. You do this not to create an antisocial environment but to create a sense of balance and harmony within the home. At various times over the years, my wife and I have felt that our home has seemed more like a train station or busy bus stop than it has a retreat. By simply acknowledging our desire to create a more peaceful environment and by making a few minor adjustments to protect our privacy, we have been able to bring that balance back into focus.

You can learn to say no more often to requests that would bring you away from your home, *and* you can learn to reduce your invitations to friends and others to enter your home. Again, you do this not to become a hermit or to alienate your friends and family but to protect and honor your need for privacy. When you do so, you'll notice a significant difference in the way you feel. You'll feel more nurtured and peaceful. And when you do invite others into your home, and when you accept those gracious invitations from others, you will do so knowing that you are doing so from a place of genuine desire rather than because you feel pressured to do so, out of obligation.

We all need some degree of privacy. When you enter your home, know that it is your own. Whether you rent a small room in someone else's house, occupy an apartment, or own your own home, honor your need for privacy. Before too long, things won't get to you as much.

6.

FORGIVE YOUR OUTBURSTS

I don't care who you are—or how together you are—there will be times when you simply "lose it." More often than not, losing it isn't all really that big of a deal. You get angry or raise your voice. You feel victimized or taken for granted. You throw up your hands in disgust. You get so stressed out that you feel like you're going to "flip out." You might even rant and rave, or worse yet, you might even punch or throw something. But, unless you actually hurt someone or yourself, it's important to forgive your outburst, admit that you're only human, move on, and vow to become less uptight. That's the best you can do.

A bigger problem, I believe, than a outburst is the way we beat ourselves up after the fact. We tell ourselves what bad people we are, or what a bad job we're doing at home. We feel guilty and fill our minds with negativity and self-pity. Sadly, this self-defeating inner talk doesn't accomplish anything positive—and may even actually encourage us to *repeat* the very behavior we are upset about by keeping our attention and focus on the problem.

Throughout my career, I've met some extraordinary people, including a number of world-famous therapists and authors who special-

17

ize in teaching others to be peaceful. While most of them are, in fact, peaceful and loving people, not one of them, by their own admission, is exempt from an occasional outburst of frustration. Everyone is human and deserves to be forgiven. Especially you!

Becoming a more peaceful person, especially around the familiarity of the home, is a process, not a destination. It's common for people to say to me, "I've learned to be a far less reactive person and I'm a great deal happier than ever before, but I still lose it once in a while." My response is almost always, "Congratulations! You're doing great."

One of the keys to forgiving yourself quickly is to admit that you lost it and to remind yourself that you will certainly do so again— probably thousands of time. It's okay. The more important piece of the puzzle is that you're moving in the right direction. And when you start to forgive your own outbursts, it will become far easier to extend the same courtesy to others as well. In fact, in our home I sort of like it (once in a while) when one of the kids, or Kris, loses it a bit because it gives me a chance to practice compassion and reminds me that, essentially, we're all in this together. After all, I know all too well how bad it feels. My guess is that if you can be more forgiving of your own outbursts and those of others, the downs you experience and your tendency to sweat the small stuff at home will lessen substantially.

7.

LISTEN TO HER (AND HIM TOO)

If I had to pick a single suggestion that was designed to help virtually all relationship and family problems, it would be to become a better listener. And although a vast majority of us need a great deal of work in this area, I'd have to say that it's us *men* who need it the most!

Of the hundreds of women I've known over my lifetime, and the thousands I've spoken to through my work, a vast majority complain that a spouse, boyfriend, significant other, or father is a poor listener. And most say that the slightest improvement in the quality of listening would be extremely well received and would undoubtedly make the relationship, regardless of the nature of the relationship, even better. Listening is almost like a "magic pill" that is virtually guaranteed to produce results.

It's interesting to speak to couples who claim they have a loving relationship. In most cases, if you ask them the secret of their success, they will point to the other person's ability to listen as one of the most significant factors that contributes to the quality of their relationship. This is also true of positive father/daughter, as well as boyfriend/girl-friend, relationships.

Why, then, if the payback is so powerful and certain, do so few of us become good listeners? There are a few reasons that stick out in my mind. First, as far as men are concerned, many of us feel that listening is a nonproactive solution. In other words, when we're listening instead of jumping in, we don't feel as though we're doing anything. We feel we're being too passive. It's hard for us to accept the fact that the listening itself is the solution.

The way to overcome this particular hurdle is to begin to understand how much being listened to is valued by the people we love. When someone genuinely listens to us, it feels as though we are heard and loved. It nourishes our spirits and makes us feel understood. On the other hand, when we don't feel listened to, our hearts sink. We feel as though something is missing; we feel incomplete and dissatisfied.

The other major reason so few of us become good listeners is that we don't realize how bad we really are! But, other than someone telling us about it or pointing it out to us in some way, how would we know? Our poor listening skills become an invisible habit that we don't even realize we have. And because we have so much company, our listening skills probably seem more than adequate—so we don't give it much thought.

Determining how effective you are as a listener takes a great deal of honesty and humility. You have to be willing to quiet down and listen to yourself as you jump in and interrupt someone. Or you have to be a little more patient and observe yourself as you walk away, or begin thinking of something else, before the person you are speaking to has finished.

This is about as close as you're going to get to a virtually guaranteed result. You may be amazed at how quickly old problems and issues correct themselves and how much closer you will feel to the ones you love if you simply quiet down and become a better listener. Becoming a better listener is an art form, yet it's not at all complicated. Mostly, all it requires is your intention to become a better listener, followed by a little practice. I'm sure your effort will be well worth it!

8.

MAKE PEACE WITH BICKERING

There's nothing quite like a bickering match between siblings to ruin an otherwise peaceful day around the house. Anyone who has experienced sibling rivalry knows exactly what I mean.

It was shortly after our youngest daughter's second birthday when one of my friends suggested "You'd better get used to it" in response to my concern about squabbling that seemed to be brewing. It turns out she was absolutely right. The truth is, if you have more than one child, bickering is a fact of life. The question isn't whether or not bickering will occur but instead: What is the best and wisest strategy to deal with it?

I'm the first to admit that there are times when bickering gets on my nerves in a big way. However, I have found that the best strategy available to parents, grandparents, baby-sitters, caretakers—anyone dealing with kids and bickering—is to make peace with it, once and for all. I realize this is easier said than done, but what options do you really have?

There are two excellent reasons for making peace with bickering. The first is that when you struggle against something—anything—it makes whatever you are struggling against seem even worse than it really is. For example, if your two sons are arguing and you get overly involved, intervene too quickly, or become too reactive, you have to deal with not only fighting kids but your own reactions as well—high blood pressure, negative thoughts, and agitated feelings. When you struggle against bickering it's as if you enter the ring with your kids. This makes it easy to blow the bickering out of proportion, which is another way of saying you'll end up sweating the small stuff.

The second reason to make peace with bickering is that when you struggle against it, you actually encourage more of the same. In a way, you're sending the wrong message, even acting as a poor role model. After all, how can you be demanding "peace" from your children when you are experiencing conflict? In most cases, your kids will sense your agitation and reactivity, which encourages each child to see if he or she can convince you to take sides. Your inner struggle (or external reactions) further fuel the fire.

The good news is, the opposite is equally true. When you make peace with bickering, when you accept it as part of the package of parenting, no added fuel is thrown on the fire. In fact, there is a relationship between the degree to which you can stay detached and relaxed and a lesser amount of bickering that you will have to endure.

Obviously, there are times when you'll want or have to get involved, and, of course, you'll want to guide your children in their journey toward getting along with one another. What I'm referring to are the ongoing bickering matches that exist on a day-to-day basis. These everyday, normal conflicts are the ones that you want to make peace with. As is so often the case, our acceptance of what is, instead of our insistence that life be what we would like it to be, is the key to a more peaceful life. When you make peace with bickering, you set an example of choosing not to participate or overreact to strife and chaos. My guess is this: If you can become a tad bit more detached from, and make peace with, normal sibling bickering, your kids will quickly follow suit.

9.

THINK OF TAKING CARE OF YOUR
HOME LIKE PAINTING THE BRIDGE

An architect once told me something that truly amazed me about the amount of work it took to maintain the Golden Gate Bridge in the San Francisco Bay Area. He said the bridge is painted virtually every day of the year. In other words, by the time the work is done, it's time to start over. It's never done! Instead, it's literally an ongoing process. Furthermore, in the absence of this constant care, the bridge would be in jeopardy of expensive wear and tear as well as more cosmetic consequences.

One day it dawned on me that taking care of a home is much like painting this extraordinary bridge. And thinking of it in these terms has been an enormous relief in my life.

Like most people, I used to get overwhelmed about the care and maintenance of our home. If something was in need of repair or disorganized, it would make me nervous and frustrated. Looking back, it seems that I was frustrated most of the time, because it seemed like something was always wrong with our home—a sink needed repair, a room needed paint, the attic needed cleaning, the dishes needed to be washed, a closet was a mess, weeds needed to be pulled, and so forth. It was as if I felt that there would come a time when it would somehow all be done. And, I fantasized, when it was finally finished, I'd be able to feel relaxed and satisfied.

Well, several years later, the house is still "in process." The weeds still need to be pulled, the attic still gets messy, dishes are still in the sink, and my daughters' rooms need paint once again! In a way, it's exactly like the Golden Gate Bridge. It's never done—and it never will be. The only difference is that now I understand and have accepted this fact about having a home.

Looking at my home in this way has been a tremendous relief. Now, instead of panicking or overreacting when something isn't finished or needs to be done, I'm able to keep it in much better perspective. I'm not suggesting that I don't work hard to keep things in good repair and orderly—I do, only I'm not nearly as attached to completing the project.

My guess is that if you look at your home in this way it will be a tremendous source of relief. In all likelihood, you'll have even greater appreciation for the things that do get finished and less frustration over those things that don't.

10.

DON'T ANSWER THE PHONE

How often have you been completely overwhelmed by all that you're doing at home when, at the worst possible moment, the phone rings? Or, you're trying desperately to get out the door by yourself or with your kids when—*ring, ring ring*—the phone calls out for your attention. Or, on the other end of the spectrum, you're absorbed in a special moment—by yourself or with someone you love—when, again, the phone rings.

The question is, did you answer it? If you're like most people, you probably did. But why? Our response to a ringing phone is one of the few things in life over which we have absolute control and decision-making authority. In this day and age of answering machines and voice mail, it's not as critical to answer the phone as it once was. In most cases, we can simply call someone back at a more convenient time.

In our home, one of the most stressful moments is when the phone rings just as we are going out the door in the morning and one of the kids runs over and answers it! Now, rather than getting in the car, I'm back on the phone addressing someone else's concern. The time and accompanying stress is rarely worth it. I've learned a little secret. I have one of those phones that has a "ringer off" feature. Sometimes, when

27

I remember, I turn the ringer off about thirty minutes before we actually have to leave. This way, the kids won't be tempted to answer the phone.

Many years ago a good friend of mine and I were talking about the issue of answering the phone during a family dinner. We agreed that unless you were expecting a very important call, answering the phone during family time sends a hurtful message to your entire family and is, in fact, disrespectful. The message is: An unknown person is calling and it's more important to me that I answer his or her call than it is to sit with you right now. Pretty scary, isn't it?

Some of my most magical moments with my kids have been when we've been spending time together reading or playing and the phone rings. But rather than interrupting our time together, we look at each other and agree—nothing is more important than our time together right now! This is one of the ways I show my kids how important they are to me. They know I practically live on the phone and my decision to not answer it doesn't come easily.

Obviously there will be many times when you'll want to answer the phone. I urge you, however, to choose carefully. Ask yourself the question "Is answering the phone at this moment going to make my life easier, or is it going to add stress to my day? Simple as it seems, choosing *not* to answer the phone, on selected occasions, can be a very empowering decision and can greatly reduce the stress in your home life.

11.

LIVE FROM YOUR HEART

A subtle yet major contributor to sweating the small stuff for many people is the failure to live from the heart. Instead, many people fall into routines out of default, or because everyone else seems to be doing something, or because it *seems* like the right thing to do. For example, people often choose careers that their parents wanted for them, or because of some perceived status or some other external measure. Or some parents will put their kids into certain activities or dress them in certain clothes simply because everyone else is doing it. Still others will struggle to buy a home instead of renting an apartment because they heard it was part of the American Dream, or they will, in some other way, live beyond their financial means because they are trying to "keep up with the Joneses."

Living from your heart means that you choose a life and a lifestyle that are true for you and your family. It means you make important decisions because they resonate with your heart and your own values, and not necessarily with those of others. Living from your heart means that you trust your own instincts more than the pressures from advertising or the expectations of society, neighbors, and friends.

Living from your heart, however, does not mean you become a

rebel, break family tradition, or become different from everyone else. It's far more subtle than that. Living from the heart is about trusting that quiet voice within you that emerges when you quiet down enough to listen. It's that voice that speaks to you from a place of wisdom and common sense instead of from frantic chatter and habit. When you trust your heart rather than your habits, new insights will pop into your mind. These insights can be anything from the idea to move to a different town, to the realization of the necessity to break a destructive habit, to an answer of how to communicate differently with someone you love. You might also have insights about who you choose to spend time with as well as new ways to solve problems. It all starts from listening to your heart.

A failure to live from the heart creates a great deal of internal conflict, which in turn encourages you to become short-tempered, easily bothered, and reactive. Deep down, you know what is true for you, what kind of life you want to be living, and what type of person you want to be. If your actions are inconsistent with your deeper wisdom, however, you will feel frustration and stress. As you learn to live from your heart, these tendencies will gradually fade away and you will become calmer, happier, and less stressed. You will be living *your* life instead of everyone else's.

The way to live more from your heart is to commit to doing so. Ask yourself questions like: "How do I really want to live my life?" "Am I following my own path or am I doing things simply because I've always done them that way, or because I'm living up to someone else's expectations?" Then simply quiet down and listen. Rather than trying to come up with an answer, see if you can allow the answers to come to you, as if out of the blue.

If you want to become more peaceful, and a whole lot happier, this is a good place to start. Living from your heart is one of the foundations of inner peace and personal growth. It will encourage you to be kinder and a great deal more patient. Give it a try. You'll be surprised, even delighted, at what you might discover.

12.

KEEP YOUR PROMISES

In my opinion, no book on improving family life would be complete without at least a few words on keeping your promises. This is an extremely powerful, long-term strategy to keep you permanently bonded with those you love. You can do a lot of things wrong, but if you keep your promises, you'll be richly rewarded in terms of the quality of your relationships and the integrity that others will perceive that you will have. On the other hand, if you fail to keep your promises, those around you—even your own family—will take your words less seriously, or even worse, learn to distrust you altogether.

Obviously, no one is perfect, and there will be times when you fail to keep a promise for a variety of reasons—you'll forget, or something "pressing" will come up. In most cases this isn't a problem because keeping your promises isn't an all-or-nothing proposition but a lifetime process. In other words, your goal isn't to be perfect but to strive to keep as many of your promises as possible.

Not too long ago, I had promised to attend my daughter's soccer game, but a few weeks later was given the opportunity to appear on a major national talk show to discuss *Don't Sweat the Small Stuff*. All things considered, I needed to go. My daughter was truly disappointed. I felt like a successful parent, however, when she gave me a hug through her tears and said, "It's all right, Daddy. This is the very first game you've missed this year." My record wasn't perfect, as it rarely is, but it was pretty darn good. My daughter knew that when I said "I really wish I could be there," my words weren't hollow. She knew that my promises are important to me and I try really hard to keep them. Like most people, she doesn't expect perfection, only an honest attempt to live with integrity, to do the best I can.

It's also important to keep your more subtle or implied promises. If, for example, you tell your mother, "I'll give you a call tomorrow," make every attempt to do so. So often we will say things—make subtle promises—because it makes the moment a little easier or makes someone feel special for the time being, but we fail to deliver, thus more than erasing the positive effects of our good intentions. We'll say things like "I'll swing by later this afternoon" or "I'll be there no later than six o'clock." But, time and time again, we don't actually come through. We rationalize not keeping our promises by saying things like "I tried, but I'm really busy," but that is of little consolation to someone who is on the receiving end. To most people, a broken promise is more evidence that promises don't mean very much.

I have found that it's much better not to make a promise, even if you want to, unless you're relatively certain you'll be able to keep it. If you're not certain you're going to actually do something for someone, don't say you are going to. Make it a surprise instead. Or if you're not sure you're going to call, don't say you *are* going to call, and so forth.

By keeping our promises, we do our little part in helping our loved ones keep their cynicism to a minimum. We teach them that some people can be trusted and are trustworthy. You may be pleasantly surprised at how much people will appreciate you when you do what you say you are going to do, when you keep your promises. Your life at home and around your family will be greatly enhanced.

13.

BUY SOMETHING NEW,
LET SOMETHING GO

If you live alone, this strategy is simple. If you have a spouse or live-in partner, it's considerably more difficult. If you have a family, it's more difficult still. However, regardless of your living situation or how many people live in your home, this strategy is well worth the effort and pays tremendous dividends in terms of a more manageable, organized lifestyle.

The rationale for this concept is derived from the almost universal tendency to fill our homes to the brim. This seems to be an issue for people regardless of income, the size of their home, geographic location, race, or religion. The problem is that overcrowding can create a great deal of stress and frustration in terms of knowing where to put things and where to find them. Feeling "closed in" can also have a negative impact on your psyche, making it easier to feel stressed and irritable.

The truth is, most people fill up their existing storage space to its absolute capacity. If you have two closets in your apartment, each of them is undoubtedly full. If you have three, they are probably full as well. Regardless of how much storage space any of us has, we seem to find a way to fill it. And of course, this would be okay if we never again bought or received a single new item that takes up space. But, alas, this is surely not the case. Most of us are constantly taking in new and used items on a consistent basis.

The question is, where do we put it all? What most of us do is rearrange our existing "stuff" to make room for the new. Rather than get rid of things, we try to reorganize, cram things together, and pile items on top of one another. We fill up our attics, garages, shelves, and other storage spaces. A few people even rent storage units at outside locations to create the needed room. We collect things for many reasons—fear of needing them someday, habit, and nostalgia.

The solution, while requiring a bit of discipline, is quite simple and is virtually 100 percent effective. Once you recognize that you are operating at full capacity, what you need to do is make a vow that as one new item is brought into the home, something else must go. For example, suppose your five-year-old daughter receives two new teddy bears for her birthday. Using this strategy, you and your daughter would have to decide which of her comparable toys would need to be given away in order to create the necessary space to keep the new bears. Implementing this strategy does several things. First, it keeps the amount of "stuff" in your home completely under control. You are constantly creating space for new things by removing things that you no longer need or use. A hidden benefit here can be a greatly reduced cost of living. This strategy encourages you to think twice about buying new things because you know you have to get rid of something else. In addition, you are setting an example to your child that it's important that we share our things with other people, perhaps those less fortunate than ourselves. We can explain that many children have no toys and that we can give a few of our things away to make their lives brighter. The same principle applies whether we are taking in new teddy bears, furniture, Tupperware, or clothing.

Obviously, there are plenty of exceptions to this rule. If you don't have enough furniture in your home, it would be silly to get rid of things that you actually need simply because of an overly rigid commitment to this or some similar plan. Or, if you truly need or want a new pair of jeans, or if your child has only a few toys, you don't need to take this strategy literally. However, in many instances, I think you'll agree that we do have all that we truly need. In these instances, I think you'll find this strategy is one you'll learn to love. You'll enjoy the fact that your home isn't overly cluttered regardless of how much new stuff comes your way—and you'll enjoy knowing that other people who truly need things are using those things that would have only been taking up space in your closet. This is a simple, highly effective solution to an almost universal problem.

14.

ENCOURAGE BOREDOM

IN YOUR CHILDREN

To the typical parent, little is more aggravating than hearing these words from their children: "I'm bored" or "There's nothing to do." This is especially true for parents who try really hard to provide their children with a variety of experiences and activities to choose from. Yet, ironically, it's the parents who try the hardest who usually suffer the most from these words.

Children who have too many opportunities, choices, scheduled activities, and things to do are often the ones who are the most susceptible to boredom. The reason is that these children are used to being entertained and stimulated virtually every moment of every day. They often rush from activity to activity with little time in between and have schedules that look almost as full as those of their parents! Very simply, if something isn't going on, they feel bored and restless, almost desperate to find something to do. Many kids feel they can't live without a telephone in their hand, a television set or radio playing at virtually every moment, or a computer or video game to entertain them.

The solution *isn't* to feed them ideas of things that they can do to alleviate their boredom. As you know, they will usually reject your ideas anyway. A bigger issue, however, is that in the long run you're doing a disservice to your kids. By offering too many suggestions about ways to keep busy, you are actually feeding the problem by suggesting that the kids really *do* need something to do every minute of every day.

A great solution (and one that will shock your bored kids) is to respond to the "I'm bored" line with a confident "Great, be bored." You can even go on and say "It's good for you to be bored once in a while." I can almost guarantee you that, once you try this a few times and really mean it, your kids will give up on the idea that it's *your* responsibility to entertain them on an ongoing basis. A hidden benefit to this strategy is that it will encourage greater creativity in your kids by forcing them to discover things to do on their own.

I'm not suggesting you do this all the time or that you don't take a loving, active role in the activities that your kids participate in. What I'm referring to here is a response to overstimulation—when you know in your heart that your kids have plenty of things to do and that their boredom is coming from them, not from a lack of possibilities. I think you'll love the sense of authority you'll feel by putting the problem of boredom back where it belongs—with your kids. And, as important, you'll be doing your kids a tremendous favor by teaching them that there's nothing wrong with not having something to do every minute of every day. It's okay to be bored once in a while.

15.

EXPECT IT TO SPILL

I learned this trick more than twenty years ago. It has proven day after day, year after year, to be extremely effective in my goal of creating a more peaceful home environment for myself and for others.

The basis for this strategy stems from the understanding that when we expect something to occur, we are less surprised and therefore less reactive to it. In addition, when we expect something to happen—that is, when we expect something to spill—and it doesn't, we feel grateful. In other words, we begin to appreciate the fact that, a vast majority of the time, the things we are eating and drinking don't get all over the floor and, most of the time, life does go smoothly. The problem is, we tend to focus on the annoying exceptions.

Think back to the last time you or someone in your family spilled a glass of milk or a cup of coffee on the carpet. What was your reaction? In all probability, it involved panic, disappointment, and a great deal of stress. What do you suppose would happen if, instead of assuming that nothing should or will ever spill, you instead expected the beverage to spill—you accept it as inevitable? It puts an entirely different slant on the same set of facts. This doesn't mean you like it when the spill occurs, only that it's okay when it does—you accept it. Obviously, you have no idea when the spill is going to occur, only that, in all likelihood, it will at some point. It might be later today, next week, or three years from now, but unless you are a rare exception, you will have spilled milk in your home at some point in the future. This strategy prepares you for this inevitable moment.

The same metaphor can easily be extended to virtually any other likely daily annoyance at home—something doesn't work right, something breaks down, some big mess occurs, someone doesn't do his or her part, whatever! The point is, when you expect something to happen, it won't come as such a surprise when it does. Don't worry that by expecting something to happen you're going to encourage it to take place. You're not. We're not talking about "visualizing" something to happen or encouraging it in any way. We're referring here to the gift of acceptance, learning to accept things as they are instead of pinning our happiness on the way we demand things to be. Watch what happens when you expect something to spill. I'll bet you'll find yourself far more relaxed the next time it occurs.

16.

ALLOW "WHITE SPACE"
IN YOUR CALENDAR

Too much of anything, even good things, is just that—too much! Regardless of how social you are—or how much you love spending time with others—there is something magical and peaceful about looking at your calendar and seeing white space, *un*-planned-for time. "White space" is time for you to catch up, or to do nothing at all. Creating blocks of time in your calendar where absolutely nothing is planned contributes to a feeling of peace, the feeling that you have enough time.

If you wait for everything to get done before you allow time for yourself, you'll rarely, if ever, find it. Instead, your calendar and schedule will miraculously fill up with your own commitments, as well as with the needs and requests of others. Your spouse or partner will have things for you to do, your kids (if you have them) will have no trouble firing requests at you, as will the neighbors, your friends, and family. Then there are the social commitments—some you love, others agreed to out of obligation. Many other requests, of course, come at you from work as well as from strangers such as telephone solicitors and sales-people. It seems that everyone wants and gets a piece of your time. Everyone, that is, except you.

The *only* solution seems to be to schedule time for yourself with the same degree of respect and commitment that you would schedule an appointment with your doctor or best friend. You make an appointment and, short of an emergency, you keep it! The procedure itself is very simple. You look at your calendar and schedule (in pen) time for yourself. You need to cross out blocks of time where you don't allow anything to be formally scheduled.

As I look at my own calendar, I'm noticing that I have time for myself scheduled this Friday between 1:30 and 4:30 P.M. There is *nothing* scheduled during that time and, short of an emergency, nothing will be. This means that when someone asks me to do something during that time block—a radio show wants an interview, someone wants me to call, a client needs my help, whatever—I can't do it. I've already got plans! And those plans are with myself. Later this month, I have an entire day blocked out. This too, is sacred time, and I can almost guarantee that it won't be filled up.

As you can imagine, this takes some getting used to. When I first started scheduling time for myself a few years back, I used to have the fear that, as I was taking time for myself, I was missing out on other opportunities or that I would be perceived as selfish. It was very difficult for me to learn to say that I didn't have time when there was that opening in my calendar! What I realized, however, was that I was worth it—and so are you.

This white space time has become one of the most important scheduled activities on my calendar and is something I have learned to protect and value. This doesn't mean my work is any less important to me, or that my time with my family isn't still the most important activity of all. Instead, it simply suggests that my white space time creates a needed degree of balance that nurtures my soul. Without it, life seems too hectic and overwhelming.

I encourage you to start today. Take a look at your calendar and pick a regular time—once a week, even once a month to begin with—even if it's just a few hours, but reserve some time for yourself. Then, as requests come your way, don't even think about putting them in this sacred time slot. Begin to value your time as much as, or more than, anything else. Don't worry. You won't be turning yourself into a selfish person. In fact, just the opposite is likely to occur. As you begin to feel as though your life is your own again, you'll find that you're far more available to the needs of others. When you finally have what *you* need, you'll discover it's easier to give back to others.

17.

DON'T WAIT FOR BAD NEWS TO

APPRECIATE YOUR LIFE

Eventually, many of us will receive a much-dreaded terminal diagnosis. And besides the shock that we will undoubtedly experience, one other thing is certain to occur: Our ordinary life will be experienced with heightened appreciation. The things we sometimes take for granted—laughter, beauty, friendships, nature, family and loved ones, our home—will all seem more important and special than ever before. Each day will be experienced as a gift and as a cherished miracle. What's more, all the "small stuff" that tends to bother us so much won't seem at all important or worthy of so much attention. The little aggravations that we tend to focus on will fade in significance. Our attention will be on the tremendous gift of life.

Because we know, with relative certainty, that this will be our reaction to bad news, as it has been for so many before us, what possible value could there be in *waiting* to appreciate your life? Instead of postponing your experience of gratitude until you are forced to do so by some form of bad news, why not instead begin to treasure your life right now? Life itself is a miracle, and we are truly blessed to be here.

A great deal of potential enlightenment can be found by reminding yourself how short and fragile life really is and how quickly things can change—one minute you have a spouse or a child, the next you don't. One minute you think you're going to live forever—the next you discover you will not. One day you enjoy your daily walk—the next you have an accident that makes walking impossible. One day you have a home—the next it's lost in a fire. You get the picture. Obviously there are two distinct ways to look at the uncertainty and fragility of life. One way is to feel defeated and frightened over the inevitability of change, including painful changes. The other, more positive, take on the same set of facts is to use this uncertainty as a constant reminder to be grateful.

Because we are so familiar with, and spend so much time at, our homes, it's easy to take for granted our families, possessions, environment, privacy, safety, comfort, and all the other things our homes provide us with. Because of this tendency, it's critical to constantly remind ourselves of how fortunate we are to have a home, however humble it may be. We need to take actual time (perhaps a few minutes) every day to think about and express, if possible, gratitude for the important role our homes play in our lives. Instead of waiting for bad news to make you treasure the gift of your life, if you begin to make it an integral part of your life right now, you'll experience more joy around the home than you ever felt possible. Give it a try. I'll bet you have a lot more to be grateful for than you realized.

18.

MAKE LIGHT OF BEING

OVERWHELMED

The other day, my wife, Kris, and I broke out into one of those belly laughs—the kind where you're laughing so hard that you start to cry. Kris said something to the effect of "This has got to be some sort of a divine joke." She was referring to the fact that the two of us had spent several hours picking up the house, putting things away, organizing, and so forth. But, despite our valiant, focused efforts, it was obvious that we were actually moving backward!

No, we're not incompetent. In fact, we're both quite skilled (and practiced) at keeping things clean and neat. The fact was, however, that each of our children had a friend over. One of the kids had tracked mud through our kitchen while Kris was busy cleaning out the closet. (The guilty party had obviously forgotten our "shoes off" policy.) A couple of other kids had been trying to get something out of our daughter's closet when—*bam*—half the toys fell all over the floor. Meanwhile, I was up in the attic attempting to put into boxes some things we were going to give away, when my foot went right through the floor, creating a large hole in the ceiling of the room below. There seemed to be chaos in every room. It was clearly "one of those days." You've undoubtedly had similar experiences at your home.

At times like these, it's tempting to get really serious and upset. For many of us, there's an almost certain knee-jerk reaction of telling yourself how unfair life is and convincing yourself how useless your efforts are. Frequently, during stressful and frustrating times like these, we mentally review how many times this has happened in the past and how likely it is to occur in the future. Needless to say, however, none of this mental rehearsal does the least bit of good.

One of the more effective ways of dealing with being overwhelmed is to step back from the situation and see the humor. As Kris pointed out, "If someone were secretly watching this scene, they would be in hysterics, laughing at us!" It was at that point that we both lightened up about the whole scenario.

Does this mean we didn't care about the mess? Absolutely not. If anything, Kris and I are neat freaks. Both of us prefer and love a clean, orderly home. There are times, however, when you simply don't have control over your environment—especially if you have one or more children. Sometimes there are too many people in your living space, or too many things going on, or not enough time, or whatever. This isn't to suggest you shouldn't try, only to remind you that you're only human. There is just so much a person can do.

When you attempt to see the humor in your fruitless efforts, it takes the pressure off feeling as though you have to be perfect, or that you have to maintain a perfect house. Instead of scrambling out of frustration to "get it all done," you might be able to come to peace with the fact that, even if you dust the last table, it will probably be dusty again in a day or so. Humor doesn't keep your house clean or organized, but it does give you perspective and make you feel better. Without minimizing its importance, it does remind you not to take your chores and responsibilities too seriously.

19.

ASK YOURSELF THE QUESTION
"WHAT MESSAGES AM I REALLY
SENDING TO MY CHILDREN?"

One of my favorite parenting books is Dr. Wane Dyer's *What Do You Really Want for Your Children?* In it, he encourages parents to ask themselves what they really want to teach their kids and to examine the hidden messages we are sending them. He suggests that some of the most important and valued human qualities—self-reliance, risk taking, patience, independence—can be hampered by the invisible ways we communicate with our kids.

Sometimes, for example, we demand that our children relax, or quiet down, but do so by raising our own voices in frustration. Or, we want our kids to grow up being independent, yet we clean their rooms out of personal frustration, or fail to allow our children to take appropriate risks. Perhaps we *say* we want our children to be calm, yet we are hyper, even frantic, ourselves. Perhaps we want our children to grow up being cooperative, yet we have a tendency to argue too often. There are many examples where we want to encourage a certain type of behavior yet we are sending a message that suggests otherwise.

So many of the messages we send our kids stem from what's going on inside of us. Are we frustrated and reactive—or are we calm and responsive? Are we patient and supportive or demanding and aggressive? Are you a great listener? Do you listen to your spouse, your friends, and your kids, or do you have a tendency to interrupt others or finish their sentences? If so, is it any wonder why our children have difficulty paying attention to and/or listening to our instructions?

One of the positive hidden messages Kris and I have given to our children is that we have made the conscious decision to always keep our own relationship alive and fresh. We make plenty of time for each other and go out on regular dates. In addition to enjoying our relationship, we want our children to grow up *knowing* that their parents truly love and value each other—not just because we tell them so but because we demonstrate with our actions and behavior what a good relationship looks like. One of the things I think we need work on is our tendency to rush, yet ironically, we get annoyed when our kids are impatient. Again, the behavior in the home is affected by the hidden messages we send our kids.

Take a look at your own hidden messages and signals. In all likelihood, there are many things you are doing well and other areas that may need improvement. Don't worry about it—welcome to the human race! The most important thing is to be aware of the power of your hidden messages. Once you are, you can catch yourself when you are sending a message that is inconsistent with what you might actually desire. With a little practice in this area, I think you'll agree that asking yourself "What messages am I really sending to my kids? is an important question indeed.

20.

APPRECIATE THE TEEN PHASE

On the surface, this suggestion may seem impossible, almost a contradiction in terms! However, when you put the teen years into a broader perspective, I believe it's not only possible but in fact practical (and wise) to appreciate rather than struggle against the teen phase.

The key word in this strategy is *phase*. I'd be shocked if anyone reading this book who is at least twenty years old is the same person he or she was in their teens. More likely, you have changed your values, attitude, physical appearance, work ethic, goals, and priorities. Personally, I don't even resemble the person I was way back when I was a teen. I look different and act differently, and everything in my life has changed. I'm a completely different person—and so are you. Looking back, it was just a phase we all went through.

Why then, if we know that the teen years are just a phase, do we take it all so personally? In part, the answer to this question is that we forget that it's just a phase. We fear that the behavior and life direction of our fifteen-year-old is permanent, carved in stone. In a way, we lack the necessary faith in our teenagers. That lack of faith is felt by the youngsters of today and, I believe, contributes to some of the problems we are seeing. I'm not suggesting that if your teen is struggling it's your fault. I'm relatively certain, however, that there are things we can do to bring out the best in our teens as well as to reduce the frustration we feel.

I think that one of the reasons I came out of my teenage years relatively unscathed was that I sensed my parents' acceptance and faith in me as a person. It was as if they *knew* I was okay (even when I didn't) and that there wasn't something wrong with me simply because I was struggling. Despite the fact that my behavior was far from perfect, I knew that my parents appreciated me. Their confidence gave me the strength I needed to grow out of my phase.

Over the years I've noticed a similar dynamic in those few (lucky) homes where parents and their teens seem to thrive and live together in peace. In virtually all cases, the teens that seem to have their act together the best seem to have parents who have faith in them as people—parents who visibly appreciate their teens. Obviously, it's easy to say "Of course parents are going to have faith in (and appreciate) a teen if that youngster already has his or her act together." And perhaps there is some truth in this statement. However, I believe we can cultivate faith in and appreciation of our teens regardless of their current plight by recognizing how important it is.

You only have to ask yourself how much easier is it to perform well at anything when the people around you believe in you and when you feel appreciated. The same is true for teens. When a teen feels appreciated, he or she then has a reputation to live up to. But the reverse is also true. When a teen feels unappreciated, he or she has a reputation to live down to. I'm not suggesting this is going to be easy, only that it's important and worth factoring into your responses. If you think of the teenage years as a phase rather than something permanent, some of the struggle will ease.

21.

REFUSE TO LET IT BUG YOU

This is a fun one to practice if you have kids, but undoubtedly as effective if you do not. Refusing to "let it bug you" can apply to virtually anything—kids' fighting or demanding your attention, chaos, a messy room, a leaking roof, a noisy pet, an overflowing closet, or a snoring spouse.

Not all, but certainly part, of the problem with overreactivity stems from our habitual reactions to events that are largely beyond our control. For example, when the kids are fighting and it feels like it's going to drive you crazy, your knee-jerk reaction might be to get angry and send the kids to their rooms. Then you compound the problem by thinking to yourself, "I can't believe how often this happens," or "I can't believe how difficult it is to raise kids," or some other, equally validating statement designed to convince you that you couldn't possibly respond in any other way! In our own minds, we blow the issue out of proportion by overanalyzing and discussing it with others. Pretty soon, this and other "small stuff" starts to seem like really big stuff.

It's entirely possible to train your mind to be less reactive to ordinarily difficult events. When you refuse to let it bug you, you are not denying that something bugs you. What you *are* doing is retraining your mind to respond differently to the same set of facts. You begin by telling yourself, in advance of a normally difficult scenario, "I will not be bothered by, or overreact to, this event."

On the surface, and in the beginning, this may seem a little superficial. After all, telling yourself you're not going to be bothered can seem a little like telling yourself you feel good when you are experiencing the flu! However, if you give it a chance, I think you'll find this strategy is surprisingly effective. Be patient and give it some time. If you anticipate your own responses to life, it takes the habitual reactivity out of the picture. You will know, in advance, what your response is going to be, and you are merely using your life circumstances to practice those responses. In this way, you turn what might normally seem like a burden into an inner game.

I can't tell you how effective this has been with my own two children. Like most people, I've overreacted many times with each of my children. When I use this strategy, however, it seems to break most negative patterns that we develop through habit. Just the other day, the kids got into one of their squabbles, yelling and blaming each other. I could see it coming and silently told myself, "I refuse to be bothered by this upcoming fight." The result was one of those rare moments that every parent longs for—stunned children! I sat casually on the couch, not lifting my head from my book, even for a moment. Within two minutes the kids were absolutely silent, wondering what was wrong with me. Their dispute magically disappeared without any involvement on my part. We ended up enjoying the rest of the afternoon. You'll have fun with this one.

22.

NEVER MISS A CHANCE TO SAY

"I LOVE YOU"

In my lifetime I've heard many people complain that their parents (or their spouses) either never or seldom said (or say) "I love you." On the other end of the spectrum, I've never heard a single person complain that his or her parents, or anyone else, said these words too often.

I can't imagine anything easier than saying the words "I love you." However, for whatever reasons, many people simply don't do so. Perhaps we don't believe that our loved ones need to hear it, that they don't want to, or that they won't believe it. Or perhaps we're too stubborn or too shy. Whatever the reason, it's not good enough. There are simply too many important reasons to tell the people in your life that you love them.

Whether you heard these words enough in your own life or not is not the issue. At issue here is the fact that saying "I love you" makes people feel good. It reminds them that they are not alone and that you care. It raises their self-esteem—and it makes *you* feel good too! Undoubtedly, in my family, we do many things wrong. One thing we do right, however, is tell each other how much we love each other. It's simple, painless, and free. It's one of the most powerful sentences in the world. People who know they are loved (because they have been told) are able to offer the world their love in return. They have a quiet confidence and a sense of inner peace.

One of my firmest beliefs is that when you have what you want (in an emotional sense), your natural inclination is to give back to others. So, by saying "I love you" to a single person, you are, indirectly, helping the world at large. There is perhaps no way to guarantee that someone will feel loved and appreciated. But certainly the way to increase the odds is to tell him or her so, frequently. Genuinely saying the words "I love you" can erase many mistakes in the eyes of your loved ones. I know, for example, that when I've had difficult times with my kids, remembering to tell them I love them has helped us to forgive one another and move on.

On a more selfish note, saying "I love you" has personal benefits as well. It feels good. Since giving and receiving are two sides of the same coin, saying the words "I love you" more than makes up for not hearing them enough throughout your lifetime. It's absolutely true that giving is its own reward. And saying these loving words is one of the most basic and simple forms of giving.

There are so many opportune times to express your love in this manner—when you enter the house, right before you leave, before bed, and first thing in the morning. In our family, we have developed the habit of saying "I love you" before hanging up the telephone when we're talking to one another, as well as before we begin eating a family meal. Your opportunities are unlimited. This will be one of the easiest things you ever do—and, when all is said and done, one of the most important.

23.

DEVELOP YOUR OWN RESET BUTTONS

In every household there are warning signals that have the potential to alert us when chaos is just around the corner. The problem is, we rarely listen to these signals. Instead, we go about our business until the chaos overwhelms us. We can avoid a vast majority of this sense of being overwhelmed, however, by listening to these warning signals and learning to use them as reset buttons.

For example, one of the warning signals in our home occurs when all four of us are feeling rushed. There is an undeniable frenzied feeling that occurs when everyone feels pressured for time and seems to be rushing around, frustrated. As a family, we have learned to recognize this feeling and to treat it as a reset button. In other words, one of us will notice the feeling and say something like, "Hey, gang, here we go again," or something to this effect. This simple recognition allows us to take a breath, slow down, and in effect, start over or reset our speed. Virtually always, this warning signal is trying to tell us that we all need to slow down and regroup.

By using this reset procedure, we can regroup and regain our bearings and perspective, thereby allowing us to start over. On those occasions when we fail to listen to or pay attention to this warning signal, the feeling in our home becomes even more speeded up and usually leads to a great deal of frustration.

Other common warning signals include heated arguments between siblings. You can use the argument itself as an opportunity to reset the mood and atmosphere. Rather than waiting for a full-blown fight, take action before it gets out of control—use the early warning signs as your reset button. If you have only one child, you might consider whining in a similar light. If you live alone, a reset button might occur when there are too many items in your "in basket" or when there are too many dishes piled up in the sink. The potential list is vast, and your reset buttons will be unique. The idea is to see the stress coming before it actually arrives, to nip it in the bud.

Think about your own home for a moment. Are there predominant or recurring patterns of stress? If so, are there warning signals that precede the stress? If you look carefully, you'll probably see that there are. The trick is to use those signals to your advantage. Pay attention to them and use them as reset buttons. If you do, you'll notice far less stress in your home.

24.

EXPLORE VOLUNTARY SIMPLICITY

There is a popular, grassroots movement that is quickly gaining momentum, finding its way to many diverse groups of people. This movement is called Voluntary Simplicity. As the name suggests, it involves simplifying one's life by choice rather than out of need. It means you put a ceiling on your desires, not necessarily because you have to but because you want to—you see the wisdom and potential for peace in placing a ceiling on what you want so that you can enjoy what you already have. Simplifying your life frees up time, money, and energy so that you can have more of each for yourself and for your family.

Many people (I happen to be one of them) have found that "keeping up with the Joneses" and continuing to run on the proverbial treadmill is overwhelming and counterproductive, in addition to being stressful and time-consuming. Many of us have fallen into the habit of ever-increasing wants, needs, and desires. It seems that most of us believe that more is better—more stuff, things to do, experiences, and so forth. But is it really?

At some point, we get so busy that it prevents us from enjoying our lives. It seems that virtually every minute of every day is scheduled and accounted for. We rush from activity to activity, usually more interested in "what's next" than we are in what we're doing in the present. In addition, most of us want bigger apartments, a nicer car, more clothes, and more stuff. Whatever we have, it's never enough. Our appetite for more seems to be insatiable.

Interestingly enough, this movement toward a slightly simpler life is not limited to the superwealthy. Instead, its wisdom is seen by a wide range of people from vastly different economic circumstances. I know a number of people with very limited incomes who have chosen to embrace this philosophy, and in every case, they claim it has paid handsome personal dividends.

Sometimes, simplifying your life can involve major shifts like choosing to live in a smaller, less expensive apartment rather than struggling to pay for a larger one. This decision can make your life less stressful because it will be far easier to pay your rent. Other common decisions involve things like eating more simply, sharing and passing on clothes to others, or saying no to more opportunities to do things. The idea, of course, is to make decisions that enhance your life in the sense of making it a little easier, a little less complicated.

A few years ago I moved my office from one location to another. This seemingly simple decision had several major simplifying benefits. First, the office I moved to was far less expensive that the one I was in, therefore taking a little financial pressure off me. In addition, my new office was only a few miles from my home instead of the fifteen I was accustomed to traveling. Instead of thirty minutes or more each way, I was now driving less than five minutes. Since I probably work about fifty weeks a year, I'm saving more than two hundred hours a year on this one simple decision. Sure, I had a nicer office before, but was it worth it? Looking back, it was clearly not! Given the same opportunity, I'd make the same decision.

Buying or leasing a simpler car saves money and possibly trips to the mechanic. Having fewer things means less things to take care of, insure, think about, worry about, and keep clean. Every item you purchase on credit is more to pay for, but is also one more bill to pay each month. Having a home with a yard involves gardening and time to care for it. I could go on, but I'm sure you get the picture. Voluntary Simplicity is not about giving up everything you own. To the contrary, there are obviously certain instances when obtaining (rather than getting rid of) something makes your life easier and simpler. For example, I can't imagine giving up my computer or fax machine. To do so would clearly make my life far more complicated and difficult. In fact, without my computer, I doubt very much that you'd be reading this book right now!

Voluntary Simplicity is not about any single decision, nor is it about voluntary poverty. You can drive an expensive car and still be committed to simplicity. You can enjoy, have, and even want nice things and still enjoy a simpler life. It's more of a direction, a series of conscious decisions that you make because you want to improve the quality of your life. The key is to take an honest look at what's truly important in your life. If you'd like a little more time, a little more energy, and a little more peace of mind, I encourage you to explore this topic a little more carefully.

25.

KEEP GOOD COMPANY

Most people acknowledge the fact that we are affected positively and negatively by the people we spend the most time around. Kids are affected by their parents and vice versa, and spouses are affected by one another, as are siblings. We are also affected by the people we work with and by our friends and neighbors.

There are times, of course, when we have little or no control over who we spend time with—at work, for example. In these instances, it's often the case that we simply have to make the best of it. The same is sometimes true with certain family members. You spend time with them not only because you love them, but simply because they are family—you have no acceptable alternative.

There are other times, however, when we have absolute control over who we spend our time with. For example, our friends and people we invite into our home and talk with on the telephone.

Your time and energy are among your most precious and important assets. Therefore it's extremely important to make wise and well-thought-out choices about who you spend your time with. Do you spend time with people who are truly nourishing to you (and your family), or do you choose your company much more randomly? If you're honest, you might be surprised by your answer. Perhaps you are friends with people without really knowing why—or out of laziness, perceived convenience, or simply habit.

I'm not suggesting that you necessarily break off your friendships and form new ones. Nor am I suggesting that all friendships based on tradition, obligation, or past experience are bad or wrong. I'm simply encouraging you to reevaluate and take an honest look at how you feel when you are with someone, and shortly thereafter. Is the person you are with helping you to grow? Is he or she a person you admire and respect? Do you nourish one another? Do you share similar values? Do you feel good about the way you have spent your time in person or on the phone? If not, it doesn't mean you can't still be friends, only that you might want to make the decision to spend *less* time with that person, which will create the time and space to meet new people or to spend more time alone.

This suggestion has nothing to do with making judgments about other people. If you determine that there are people you'd rather not spend so much time with, it doesn't mean that you don't respect and honor them or that you don't think they are terrific people. It also doesn't mean that you think you are any better than them or that they don't have wonderful qualities. It simply means that, all things considered, you'd rather spend your available time either by yourself or with someone else. Keep in mind that each of us has only a certain amount of time to spend with other people, probably far less than we would like. It's up to each of us to make the best choices we can. In my life, for example, I've met hundreds of people I really like for a variety of reasons but would much rather not spend time with. And, for the most part, my guess is that most of those people feel the same way about me. I love to spend time alone, and if I'm going to be with someone else, I'd like it to be with someone I truly enjoy being with.

People have different preferences regarding the types of other people they choose to spend time with. For example, generally speaking, I'd rather not spend too much time around people who are irritable and easily annoyed. I also prefer to avoid people who like to commiserate and complain. Part of my preference has to do with the fact that I acknowledge that I'm affected by the people around me. So, if I spend time with complainers, I tend to do a little more complaining myself, and so forth.

This strategy has the potential to have a major influence on the quality of your life. The people around you, particularly those you choose to spend time with, have a great deal of influence on your attitude and state of well-being. If you choose to keep good company, your life will be easier and far less stressful.

26.

AGREE TO DISAGREE

We're all unique and see life a little bit differently. We have our own preferences, and we interpret things in our own special ways. Since we were all brought up and taught to think in certain ways, we have our own subtle ways of resolving conflicts, as well as our own theories as to why things happen. Each of us places varying degrees of significance on what's really relevant and important, and we can almost always find fault with the way someone else is thinking or behaving. We can usually validate our own versions of reality by focusing on examples that, we believe, prove us to be right. In short, the way we see life will always seem justified, logical, and correct—to ourselves.

The problem is, everyone else has the same assumption.

Our spouses, children, parents, friends, neighbors—and everyone else—are equally convinced that their versions of reality are the most accurate! It's absolutely predictable that the people in your life will not understand why you don't see things the way they do and will think that, if you did, all would be well.

Knowing this is true, why, then, do most of us continue to be frustrated and annoyed by the fact that we seem to disagree so often?

Why are we so easily bothered when someone we know or love expresses a different opinion or viewpoint, interprets something differently, or thinks we are wrong? I believe that the answer to these questions are very simple: We forget that, in a psychological sense, we all live in our own separate reality. The way we interpret life and the events around us has been influenced by a variety of factors that are completely unique to our own life. My childhood and life experiences were (and continue to be) different from yours, so my take on life is going to be slightly different. An event that annoys me might seem completely insignificant to you—and vice versa.

The trick to becoming more peaceful and less reactive is to remind yourself that it's okay that we're all a little different. Rather than being surprised by this fact of life, you can learn to expect, even embrace, it. Rather than becoming upset when someone you love disagrees with you, try saying to yourself, "Of course she's going to see this differently." Instead of becoming defensive when your interpretation of an event is different from someone else's, see if you can be grateful and delighted on those rare occasions when you do see things in the same way.

You can "agree to disagree." This doesn't mean that your own point of view is any less important or correct, only that you don't have to be so frustrated by the fact that others won't always agree with you or see things in the same light. In many instances, you may want to stand firm on your own opinions and values, and that's fine, but you can do so with genuine respect and understanding of the other person's opinion as well. When you do this, it eliminates a great deal of stress and a good number of would-be arguments. In most cases, the person you are disagreeing with will sense your heartfelt respect and will probably be less reactive toward you as well. In addition, as you incorporate this less-reactive attitude into your interactions with others, you will find yourself becoming more interested in the opinions of others, which will make you more fun to be around. You'll learn to bring out the best in others and you'll allow others to bring out the best in you! Everyone wins.

I have seen this simple shift in perspective help many marriages, friendships, and family relationships. It's very simple and makes life a lot more fun. So, starting today, see if you can agree to disagree. It's well worth the effort.

27.

DON'T PUT YOURSELF DOWN

It's sad, but true: A good percentage of us engage in the negative habit of putting ourselves down and/or being overly self-critical. We'll say (or think) things like "I'm too fat," "I'm no good," or "I never do anything right." Do you ever engage in this unnecessary, yet all-too-common tendency?

The problem with putting yourself down is that, no matter how wonderful you actually are or how many positive qualities you have, you'll *always* find verification of that which you're looking for. In other words, there is a tendency, in all of us, to find that which we assume to be true regardless of what that assumption happens to be, because our thinking, almost always, tends to be self-validating. For example, if you focus on those last five pounds you can't seem to lose, you'll always notice them as you examine your waistline; you won't admire and appreciate the fact that, overall, you're in excellent health. Or, if you tell yourself that you "hate family reunions," you'll tend to look for (and somehow always find) evidence of your displeasure at each family event. Instead of enjoying your favorite family members, you'll tend to notice Aunt Sarah's shrill voice or your brothers' annoying tendency to boast and brag. Or you'll focus on, and criticize, a member of the family who tends to drink too much; you won't marvel at the fact that, overall, your family is a group of really nice folks.

So, you can see that if you put yourself down for *any* reason whatsoever, it's absolutely predictable that you'll find evidence that you are correct, making it equally predictable that you'll contribute to decreased self-esteem and negative feelings. Putting yourself down also reinforces, rather than corrects, your imperfections by putting unnecessary attention and energy on everything that's wrong, rather than what's right, with you. An important question to consider is, Why would you do this, knowing that the only *possible* result is a more negative outlook, more negative feelings, and less appreciation for the beautiful gift of life? Putting yourself down also makes you sound, to others, as if you feel like a victim of some kind. People who regularly put themselves down are often seen by others as complainers who lack appreciation for their lives, not to mention the example they set to their children, family, and friends. I hope I'm beginning to convince you that putting yourself down is a really bad idea with some rather severe personal consequences.

Obviously, everyone has aspects of themselves that they could, or would like to, improve upon. For example, one of the *many* things I would love to do is to become far more patient. At times, I feel I'm too reactive and easily bothered (in fact, I'm certain this is the case). But this *doesn't* mean that I should beat myself up and put myself down simply because I acknowledge that I'm far from perfect. Doing so would only reinforce this problem and make me feel worse than I already do about this issue. Knowing that I have plenty of room for improvement and making the decision and personal commitment to continue working toward my goal of increased patience is the best I can do. The more forgiving and patient I am with myself, the easier it will be for me to stay on my path of growth and the more likely I am to maintain my patience with others.

Whatever issues you are working on, and whatever it is that you would like to improve about yourself, know that one of the *worst* things you can do is to berate yourself with self-criticism. Go ahead and try to improve, acknowledge your weaknesses, do whatever you can to make a change—*but* be easy on yourself. Don't put yourself down in front of others or even in the privacy of your own thoughts. No one wants to hear you put yourself down, and I hope you have begun to see how destructive this quality really is. So get over it! None of us is ever going to be perfect, but putting yourself down is not the remedy to this fact of life.

28.

STOP EXCHANGING HORROR STORIES

This strategy is particularly suited for people who live together. It's a common phenomenon for two people, whether they work away from the home or stay at home during the day, to come together in the evening and spend a great deal of time and energy exchanging "horror stories." More specifically, what I mean is that the bulk of the conversation is geared toward all the rotten and horrible things that went on during the day. Discussions include how difficult and tiring the day was, how many demands were placed on you, the irritations you had to face, the inconveniences, the bad experiences, the difficult moments, the demanding children, the insensitive bosses, and so forth. It seems many of us want to be sure that our spouses or living partners understand how difficult our lives really are.

There are several reasons why I believe this habit is a big mistake. First off, most of us have precious little time to spend each day with our loved ones. It seems to me that, if we have a difficult day, it doesn't make any sense to re-create it in the evening. The act of thinking about and discussing the negative events of the day is tantamount to re-experiencing them. This creates an enormous amount of stress and is emotionally draining.

Second, focusing too much on the negative parts of your day is self-validating. In other words, it serves to remind you of the pressures and difficulties of daily living, thereby convincing you that it's appropriate to be serious, heavyhearted, and uptight.

The simple act of eliminating, or at least reducing, the amount of energy you spend telling your horror stories has an almost instant and in some ways magical quality of making you feel better about your life. It's not that you don't have extremely difficult and serious things to deal with—we all do—it's just that commiserating with others about these difficult parts of life costs far more than it is worth. As you let go of this tendency, you'll be reminded of the better parts of life. It will be easier to remember and think about the loving and kind aspects of life, those things that went right and went well, the parts of your life that you are proud of and that nourish you. You'll also notice that when more of your attention is on the positive aspects of your day, your spouse or living partner will quickly follow suit. Most people, when they break this all-too-common habit, find that focusing on the positive is far more interesting and a great deal more fun. New doors will open in your relationship, and new interests will develop.

Please understand that I'm not suggesting that it's never appropriate or useful to share what's going on—including the worst things—with your loved ones. At times, you may want to, or even need to. There are many exceptions to this strategy. What I'm suggesting you get away from is the abuse of this tendency. Rather than making it a regular part of your evening, something you do without question on a regular basis, see if you can reduce it to an occasional thing that you discuss. Obviously, you want to be honest about your true feelings, but I've found that it can be richly rewarding to leave some of the negative behind. Before jumping in, you might ask yourself, "What is this going to accomplish?" Or you might ask, "Is sharing this information going to brighten either of our days, or is it going to bring us down? Is it going to bring us closer, make us more intimate, or is it going to be one more reminder of how difficult life can be?"

I think we all know that life can be extremely difficult and tiring. I also believe that most of us take it as a given that we must deal with hassles each and every day. The questions are, Does sharing all the gloomy details do any good? Does it have true value? And despite the fact that I'm as guilty as anyone else of abusing this tendency at times, I've found that, a vast majority of the time, sharing negativity is counterproductive at best and an interference to a quality, relaxing evening.

I encourage you to give this suggestion a try. The next time you feel like sharing information on how horrible or testing your day has been, see if you can keep it to yourself instead. My guess is that you'll discover it to be a truly healing thing to do.

29.

SET A GOOD EXAMPLE

Recently, I had a very touching experience with my six-year-old daughter that reminded me of the importance of this suggestion—to set a good example. One of the tiny ways I like to contribute to my community is to, whenever possible and reasonable, pick up trash and put it in the garbage can. I've been doing this for years and, every once in a while, I point out to my kids how important it is for all of us to do our small part to keep our streets, parks and neighborhoods clean.

The other day, Kenna and I were walking out of a coffeehouse and headed toward our car. I had noticed a bunch of trash that was on the ground. On this particular day, however, I didn't pick any up. When I reached my car, I looked around and Kenna wasn't with me. Concerned, I turned around and there she was, picking up the trash and putting it in the can. What made this episode even more priceless was her comment: "Daddy, aren't you forgetting something?"

Whether you have children or not, this strategy is an important one to keep in mind. The truth is, we are setting some kind of example, whether we know it or not. Our actions are seen by others and are factored into the consciousness of those around us. While any single action might not have much of an effect on another person, there is a cumulative effect. It's up to all of us to determine what type of example we want to set—loving, positive, and helpful; or lazy, apathetic, and selfish.

The decision to set a good example in as many aspects of life as possible helps guide your behavior and your reactions to stress. I try, for example, not to get too uptight in traffic and while waiting in long lines. I do this not only because it's a less stressful way to experience life but also because I wish to send a message to those around me that life doesn't have to be perfect in order to be happy and peaceful.

Take a look at the examples you are setting for those around you. Are they the examples you wish to send—or would you rather be sending different types? Whatever your answer, this is an important question to ask yourself. It can help you make behavioral and attitudinal adjustments that will make your life less stressful and more meaningful to yourself and to those around you.

30.

EXPERIENCE CALM SURRENDER

Calm surrender is a term I use to describe the process of "letting go" around the home and elsewhere. Simply put, it means surrendering, with grace and humility, to the chaos of life. It's a form of acceptance, of being okay with what is, of ending the struggle.

Often, we struggle against aspects of life that are largely beyond our control—noise, confusion, comments we don't approve of, lost items, rudeness, imperfections, negativity, broken pipes, clogged drains, whatever. We fight, get angry and annoyed, and wish things were different. We complain, fret, and commiserate. Yet, when you add up all this frustration, the end result is always the same: The things we are frustrated about remain as they are. No amount of gritting our teeth or clenching our fists makes the least bit of difference. In fact, it only adds fuel to the fire, often making things worse than they already are.

Calm surrender is not about giving up. Nor is it about being apathetic, lazy, or not caring. Instead, it's about appropriate acceptance, being willing to let go of our insistence that the events in our lives be any certain way or different than they actually are. The wisdom of this strategy is simple: Although you might wish things were different (or demand it), they are not. They are exactly as they are. This doesn't mean you shouldn't make changes or encourage improvements—you absolutely should do so in those instances where you feel it's important or necessary. What this strategy is addressing is the frustration that comes from not having things go your way.

The way to experience calm surrender is to start with little things. For example, while doing the dishes, you prove your humanness and drop and break a plate. Rather than yell and scream and stomp your feet, see if you can accept the moment for what it is—a moment that includes a broken dish. No big deal, no need to fret, no need to panic. Just loving acceptance for the truth of the moment. There before you, on the ground, is a broken plate. The question is: What are you going to do now? The plate is already broken. You can tense your arms and perhaps break another plate, or you can relax and see the humor in the fact that we are all so imperfect. Another example might be an interaction with your spouse. If he or she says something that might usually annoy you, see if you can respond a little differently. Instead of being bothered by your spouse's need to criticize, for example, see if you can "brush it off," love him or her in spite of the comment. Again, the comment has already been made. Your reaction to that comment is up to you. If you can change your habitual reactions to include more peaceful responses, you'll quickly see that everything will be all right, it's all okay.

In our home we have a little saying that one of the kids made up. I've always thought it's a great way to describe calm surrender. When something breaks or something goes really wrong, one of the kids will say, "Oh, well, everything happens!" In other words, what's the use of struggling?

This strategy is particularly effective when there is great chaos going on around the home. Yesterday, I was home with both kids and two of their friends. All the kids were hungry, and I hadn't yet cleaned up the last mess. The phone rang at the same moment the doorbell did. For a moment, I thought I was going to go nuts, and then I remembered to take a deep breath and let go. In that moment of chaos, the best I could do was experience calm surrender, to simply relax. And the interesting thing to me was that in this, as well as in every other instance like it that I can remember, the moment I relaxed and stopped struggling, everything began to calm down.

If you are willing to give this strategy a try, you'll be amazed at the results. The calmer you become, the easier your life will be. Rather than exacerbating negative events and bringing out the worst in other people, you'll begin to stop negativity before it has a chance to spiral any further. In time, and with a little practice, you'll begin to experience chaos in a whole new light. There will be so much less drama in your life. So, starting today, see if you can ease the chaos by experiencing calm surrender.

31.

CREATE A "SELFISH" RITUAL

It has always amused me when people have responded to my suggestion that they take care of their own needs with the question "Wouldn't that be selfish?" I'd like to take this opportunity to put that concern to rest! This strategy stems from the understanding that when you have what you need, in an emotional sense, you have plenty left over for other people and their needs.

If your goal is to become more relaxed and happy at home, one of the most helpful things you can do is to create an activity that is yours exclusively, something you do—just for you. For example, my private ritual is to get up really early in the morning before anyone else in my family. I use this time to stretch, have a quiet cup of coffee, and read a chapter or two in my favorite book. Sometimes I meditate or reflect on my life. I cherish this special ritual in my day.

Obviously, everyone is different. Some people like to squeeze a little exercise into their routine—creating a healthy ritual. Others like to browse bookstores or have a quiet cup of coffee before work. Still others like to take a warm bath or shower at a predetermined time. The point is, it's your time—a special part of the day that is reserved for you.

A ritual that I used to practice, that I've shared with many others, is that I would stop a few blocks from my home on my way home from work. I'd pull off the road in an area where there were lots of trees and plants. And for just a few minutes, I'd simply look at the beauty around me. Nothing fancy, not too much time. But just enough to give me a breather between my work life and coming home to energetic kids who wanted and deserved my attention. During those few minutes, I'd breathe deeply and remind myself how lucky I was to be going home to a loving family. I'd look in awe at the beautiful trees and plants. Then, after a few minutes, I'd start the car and drive home.

The difference in how I felt when I took this time was enormous. Rather than rushing in the door tired and grumpy, I'd feel relaxed and loving. I could tell the difference in my reception from my family as well. Apparently, they could sense my peace.

Whether you get up a little earlier, take a regular bath, or stop and smell the roses on your way home from work, do something. Create a ritual that is just for you. You'll be amazed at how much value you get out of so few minutes.

32.

IF YOU HAVE CHILDREN,
SET YOUR AGENDA ASIDE

Admittedly, this is a tough strategy to implement. Yet, if you give it a try, I think you'll see it's worth the effort. In case you haven't noticed, when you have no agenda at home (or at least less agenda), you'll usually have a better day than when you have a fixed plan that you're determined to stick to. When you are emotionally and rigidly tied to your plan, you'll almost always end up disappointed, as though you didn't complete enough items on your list. And even if you do, you'll be exhausted and perhaps resentful at how difficult it was to get it all done.

Obviously, there are times you must have an agenda and a plan, and at other times you'll have tasks you must complete and goals to attend to. But the spirit of this suggestion is what's most helpful. Try to see how your own rigidity, your mental ties to your plan, tend to stress you out. And not only that—you may discover that the more attached to your agenda you are, the less you actually get done. This is due to the fact that a rigid attitude makes it awkward, if not impossible, to shift gears and to go with the flow. When you have children to care for, it's almost impossible to know exactly what is going to occur on any given day. To flow with the changes and uncertainties requires an ability to be flexible and responsive.

Often, a wise idea is to keep your agenda on your back burner. In other words, know what it is you would *ideally* like to accomplish but let go of your attachment to getting it done. Then, when possible, gently seize the opportunities you have to work toward those goals. For example, you might have the goal of returning three phone calls, getting your car in for repair, and getting the grocery shopping done. Rather than being frustrated by the fact that you haven't had a moment to yourself to achieve any of these goals, be as patient as you can possibly be. Relax. Don't fill your mind with additional verification that you're "trapped at home" or that you're overwhelmed. Instead, keep your attention in the present moment as best you can. If you stay calm and responsive rather than agitated and hurried, you'll sense when the opportunity arises to attend to your agenda. Because you are in a responsive state of mind, you'll take advantage of any opportunities that present themselves and attend to your responsibilities in a wise and timely manner. And even if you never do get the opportunities you had hoped for on any given day, you'll be able to keep your perspective and remember, in the long run, that this will all be seen as "small stuff."

33.

FILL YOUR HOME WITH

EVIDENCE OF LOVE

There are so many distractions in life and reminders of the problems we must deal with that it's critical to counter this bombardment of negativity with evidence of love. Kris and I have found that it's relatively simple (and can be very inexpensive) to fill your home with evidence of love and happiness. And when you do, you are constantly reminded of the positive aspects of life.

Evidence of love can be anything beautiful, special to your heart, artistic, airy, or light—anything that reminds you of love, kindness, gentleness, and compassion. It can be the artwork of children, fresh-cut flowers, beautiful poetry or philosophy hanging on your wall, spiritual and loving books on your coffee table, or photographs of your loved ones. An acquaintance of mind writes positive, loving affirmations in calligraphy and tapes them to her refrigerator. Others save heartfelt letters and pin them on a bulletin board.

Comedian Steve Martin used to do a hilarious skit in which he played the banjo and sang about how difficult it is to be depressed while doing so. The banjo is so upbeat and happy sounding that, while you're playing it, it makes negativity and unhappiness seem a little silly. In a way, filling your home with evidence of love has a similar flavor to it. It's not impossible, but it's certainly more difficult, to get too worked up, stressed out, or depressed when there are signs of love and beauty everywhere you look.

In our home, we have photographs of friends, family, and spiritual people on many different walls. We regularly update, move around, and change the photos to keep them current and interesting. We also have great books that emphasize love visible in virtually every room, as well as beautiful artwork made for us by the kids. I'm certain that if I didn't have kids I'd ask friends or neighbors if I could have a few of their extras. In many families there is plenty to go around, and when you ask children if they will draw you a picture, many are honored to do so. The artwork of children is so uplifting, and is such a reminder of love, that I can't imagine not having plenty of it in my home. Our daughters also love to go outside and pick flowers from our yard and bring them into the house to put into water.

There is no specific way to go about implementing this strategy. It's simply a mind-set. Once you see the logic behind it and feel the positive effects, I'm sure you'll be hooked. There is simply no down-side to this idea. Starting today, begin filling your home with even more evidence of love. Every time you walk in the door, you'll be glad you did.

34.

DON'T LET MONEY GET YOU DOWN

Let's fact it. Most of us don't feel as though we have enough money to do the things we would really like to do—travel, fix up our homes, or buy the things we want or need. Indeed, the question doesn't seem to be whether or not we *have* the money we feel we need but what we are going to do with this fact of life. To a large degree, the way we choose to look at this issue will affect the overall quality of our life at home.

At times, it's tempting (and I've done this too) to spend more time complaining about how little money we have, and using it as an excuse to not have any fun, than going out and having fun with the money we do have. We dream about that special vacation we might or might not ever get to take, or that larger apartment we'd like to move into, but fail to do the smaller, yet equally enjoyable, things that we *can* afford to do, or make the best of the apartment we already have.

I have a good friend who has a very limited amount of money. It's amazing to me all that he has been able to do given his supply of available resources. He loves to take day trips and is inspired by camping. He has shown me some of the most beautiful photos of places I never knew existed. He has been on some of the most gorgeous hikes imaginable and the most incredible picnics ever. He enjoys rock climbing, flowers, birds, and sea life. He is one of the most inspiring and worldly people I've ever met, yet he rarely leaves the state. He has shown me that in our home state of California you can visit a beautiful, different place, within easy driving distance, every weekend—and never visit the same place twice if you don't want to. He chuckles at all the people he knows who have taken out bank loans to travel to exotic places like Europe but who have never seen a single state park right here near home. I've known my friend for over a decade and have never heard him complain *once* about a lack of money. In my mind, he's one of the "wealthiest" people on earth.

You can take this same mind-set and apply it to everything else where a lack of money *could* be seen as an obstacle. You can complain that you can't afford to move to a larger apartment or that you may never be able to buy your own home, or you can fix up your existing home in creative and inexpensive ways with the budget you already have. You can feel bad that you can't afford to buy your relatives the expensive Christmas gifts you'd like to get them, or you can feel proud of the meal or cookies you make for them or the beautiful card you took the time to pick out. It's up to each of us to decide for ourselves. Do we yearn for more and postpone our joy out of a lack of money—or do we make the best of it and keep our positive attitude intact?

Whenever we think more about what we don't have or can't do than about what we do have or can do, we create a gap between what we have and what we want. So often, this gap is the source of a great deal of stress. You can eliminate this source of stress by making the decision to stop using a lack of money to justify your unhappiness or boredom. This doesn't mean that you don't want or deserve more—or that you shouldn't try to get more. It merely suggests that, in the meantime, you enjoy as much as possible that which you already have. You may be surprised. If you put more attention on what you can do than what you can't do, one thing's for sure—you're going to have a lot more fun.

35.

START THE DAY WITH LOVE,

LIVE THE DAY WITH LOVE,

END THE DAY WITH LOVE

If any of us could master this strategy to its fullest, we would be among the great role models of humanity, right up there with the likes of Mother Teresa. Yet, as difficult as this strategy would be to master, it's worth every bit of effort you put into it.

Actually, the wisdom of this strategy is quite simple. The idea is to remind yourself frequently, throughout the day, of the importance of living your life with *love* as your absolute top priority. Something magical happens to your life when nothing is seen as more important than love. "Small stuff" is kept in its proper perspective and consciousness opens to the beauty and joy of life. Our day-to-day living begins to take on an extraordinary quality and we begin to experience what's truly most important in life.

"Start the day with love" means that when you wake up in the morning, you open your heart and remind yourself of your intent to be loving in every aspect of your life. "Live the day with love" means that your choices and actions stem from your decision to be loving, patient, kind, and gentle. It means you keep things in perspective and try *not* to take things personally or blow things out of proportion. It means you make allowances for the imperfections of others and of yourself, and that you make an effort to keep your criticisms and judgments from rising to the surface. Living the day with love suggests that, whenever possible, you will make an effort to be generous and complimentary, as well as humble and sincere. "End the day with love" means that you take a moment at the close of your day to reflect and be grateful. Perhaps you say a prayer or do a quiet meditation. You might look back on your day and review how closely your *goal* of living with love matched up with your actions and choices. You do this not to keep score, or to be hard on yourself, but simply to experience the peace associated with loving intent and to see areas where you might act even more loving tomorrow.

36.

NEVER, EVER, TAKE YOUR SPOUSE

(OR SIGNIFICANT OTHER)

FOR GRANTED

I could write an entire book on this subject. But, since I have only a few paragraphs to explain, I'll get right to the heart of the matter.

If you take your spouse for granted, it is absolutely 100 percent guaranteed to adversely affect your relationship. I've never, ever, met a single person who likes to be taken for granted—and very few who will put up with it, over the long run.

Clearly, one of the most disrespectful and destructive things we can possibly do to our spouses (or anyone) is to take them for granted. To do so is sort of like saying, "It's your job to make my life easier and my job to expect it." Ouch!

There are so many ways we take our partners for granted. Here are just a few: We take *our* roles more seriously than theirs. We think our contributions are significant and that our partners are "the lucky ones." Many of us forget to say please and thank-you—some of us never do. We fail to reflect on how lucky we are or how sad and difficult it would be to live without our spouses. Sometimes we get very demanding of our spouses or treat them much differently than we would a friend. Other times, we speak "for them" or disrespectfully about them in front of others. Some of us think we know what our spouses are thinking, so we make decisions for them. Then there is the common mistake of coming to expect certain things—a clean home or a hot meal. Or money to pay the bills, or a nice clean-cut lawn. They are, after all, our spouses. They should do these things. Finally, very few of us really listen to our spouses or share in their excitement—unless, of course, it matches something *we* are interested in. I could go on and on, but you get the point.

Is it any wonder that close to 50 percent of marriages end in divorce and that many of the rest are painful, boring, and/or less than satisfying? Hardly! It's so obvious, but for some reason we keep making the same mistake—we take our partners for granted.

The reverse is also true—almost nothing makes people feel better than feeling as though they are appreciated and valued. Think about how wonderful it felt when you first met your spouse or significant other. It was absolutely wonderful. And a major contributing factor to this feeling of love you shared was that you truly appreciated each other. You said things like "It's so nice to hear from you" and "Thank you for calling." You expressed your appreciation for everything from a simple compliment to the tiniest gift, card, or gesture of kindness. Each chance you had, you expressed your gratitude, and you never took your new love for granted.

Many people believe that it's inevitable that couples will lose their sense of appreciation for one another. Not so! Appreciation is something you have 100 percent control over. If you choose to be grateful and to express your appreciation, you will do so. And the more you do so, the more you'll be in the healthy habit of noticing things to be grateful for—it's a self-fulfilling prophecy.

My wife, Kris, is one of the most appreciative people I've ever known. She's constantly telling me how much she loves me or how lucky she is to be married to me. I try to remember to do the same because that's exactly how I feel. And you know what? Every time she expresses her appreciation toward me, I feel that much more love for her. And she assures me the same is true for her. But we don't do this as a way of getting love, but simply because we both tend to focus on how lucky we are to have one another as a friend and partner.

For example, I'll be away at a speaking engagement and Kris will leave me a sweet message telling me how grateful she is that I'm willing to work so hard for our family. About the same time, I'll leave a message with her, letting her know how grateful I am that she's willing and able to be home with our children, giving them the love they need and deserve, while I'm away. We both honestly feel that the other is making at least an equal sacrifice and that, regardless, we're on the same team. Then, when she's away and I'm home, it seems that we reverse compliments. She's grateful that I'm willing and able to be at home and I'm equally grateful that she's away making yet another contribution to our family.

Kris and I have been together for more than fifteen years, and we love each other more today than we did all those years ago. I'm absolutely certain that our decision to *not* take each other for granted is one of the major reasons why this is true. I'll bet you'll be shocked at how powerful this strategy can be if you give it a try. For the time being, forget what you are getting back and focus only on what you are giving. I believe that if you make the decision to stop taking your partner for granted, in time your spouse will begin to do the same thing. It feels good to be grateful. Try it, you'll love it!

37.

PUT A CEILING ON YOUR DESIRES

☞ This is one of the most important spiritual and practical lessons I've ever been lucky enough to learn. I say "lucky" because, without this bit of wisdom to guide your life, happiness can be an elusive experience that is going to happen "someday" rather than something you experience "along the way."

A "ceiling on your desires" means you put an end to the never-ending, ever-increasing list of wants, needs, and preferences that seem to dominate our lives, the "I'll be happy when I get one more thing" trap. In virtually all cases, without a "ceiling" your desires will be insatiable. As soon as one desire is fulfilled, another one magically takes its place. A rather typical example around the home might be: "I'll be happy when I get a larger apartment." That desire, once filled, is replaced with: "I'll be happy when we can afford to purchase a home." If you're not careful, you'll continue this process—"I'll be happy when we can buy better furniture [or landscape the yard]"—and your never-ending list will continue to grow and grow. The same principle applies to all material things—cars, clothes, equipment, and everything else.

But this habit of always wanting more doesn't apply only to material goods. It also spills over into our expectations, leaving us constantly dissatisfied. For example, your daughter kicks a goal in soccer and you immediately hope that someday she might score two goals. Or she gets all B's on her report card and you're disappointed that she didn't get straight A's. Or you're lucky enough to have a spouse who is virtually always very punctual. The one time he shows up late, however, you feel let down and perhaps give him a hard time rather than saying, "Don't worry about it, you're almost always on time." Or you cook an excellent meal and wonder why it's not even better. You get the point. It applies to virtually everything.

When you put a ceiling on your desires, what you are doing is reminding yourself that you can be happy—now—before you get everything you think you want or need. It also reminds you of the trap of never-ending desires, which encourages you to focus more on what you have and less on what you want, which is the basis of gratitude. And gratitude leads to happiness and contentment. A ceiling is a self-imposed, casual, flexible, nonlegal binding agreement you have with yourself that you won't spend your life always wanting life to be better!

Occasionally, when I discuss this topic in public, someone misinterprets what I mean and says, "What's the matter, don't you believe in capitalism?" Or "Don't you think we all deserve to improve our standard of living?" The answer in both cases is an absolute yes! I believe wholeheartedly in capitalism, and I believe you and I both deserve nice things *and* a good quality of life. There is absolutely nothing wrong with improving your standard of living, buying a new outfit, or moving to a larger apartment, or whatever. Or someone will say, "Don't you think we should strive for excellence and/or encourage our family members to do the same?" Again, the answer is yes. I think it's admirable to do your best and to always be attempting to do even better. I also try to encourage my own kids to do the same. Again, however, there's an enormous distinction between doing your best and always *demanding* that life be better than it already is, or having a prerequisite that things be different or better before you allow yourself to feel satisfied—with your life or with other people.

What I'm talking about is the constant, relentless, insidious habit of always wanting more and still more—more things, perfection, or whatever—and convincing yourself that you'll be happier as a result. Obviously, only you can determine what's appropriate for you, but I can assure you that *every* single decision or demand you make involving a higher quality object, an increased standard of living, or more perfection on your part or on the part of someone else will be very easy to justify. It will *always* seem like "one more" thing or "one more" demand will do the trick—then you'll be happy. It takes a great deal of wisdom to say "More isn't always better," "More isn't going to make me happier," or "I have enough."

I'm confident that if you experiment with this strategy you will discover a route to contentment that you might never have considered. You can still have a wonderful life and all the things you need—and most of what you want. However, your life will be far simpler and easier to manage. You will feel far less stress and pressure, as though a better life is just around the corner. You will spend less time thinking about what you want, you'll be less consumption oriented, and you will be much more easily satisfied. You'll also be far less inclined to "sweat the small stuff" because you will have reduced your habit of thinking that things aren't good enough as they are. Not a bad list of benefits. I hope you'll give this strategy a try. It might change your perspective a great deal.

38.

LET THEM WIN AN ARGUMENT

FOR A CHANGE

"Them" can be anyone—your kids, spouse, parents, friends, or roommates. The premise of this strategy is to show you that it's no big deal to let someone else be "right" or to win an argument. In fact, it's a stress reducer. When someone else "wins," it doesn't mean you "lose." In fact, allowing someone else to feel as though he or she has been listened to with genuine respect is, in many instances, far more satisfying than trying to cram your point of view down someone else's throat—or spending mental energy trying to convince someone else that you are right and that he or she is wrong.

The truth is, from the perspective of quality living, no one really wins an argument. When there is friction between people, the interaction is far from ideal. An argument is nothing more than two or more people trying to prove a position. Invariably, it leaves all parties feeling bad. In an argument, rarely does anyone listen or learn anything. Feelings of resentment, anger, frustration, and stress often result from the confrontation. However, when you allow someone else to win an argument, it's often the case that you *both* end up winners. Your rapport is enhanced, and your relationship has a chance to grow.

When you refuse to engage in an argument, not out of stubbornness or righteousness, but out of love and kindness, you'll see how quickly issues naturally resolve themselves. When someone begins an argument or heated discussion, you are faced with an interesting (and sometimes difficult) decision that you must make very quickly. Do you jump in or do you back off? Do you try to prove yourself and your opinion, or can you allow the other person to win or make his or her point?

Sometimes, one of my kids will say something that, on the surface, seems incorrect or unfair. One of them might, for example, say something like "You never spend any time with me." My impulse might be to argue about the comment, responding with a statement like "Yes I do. I spend lots of time with you. Don't you remember, just yesterday we went to the park and out to lunch?" What I have found, however, is that my willing participation in the argument does nothing more than keep it alive by feeding it with attention. Sometimes, a better response is something like "You're right. I hope we'll start spending more time together. I love you so much." A response such as this not only ends the argument before it has a chance to build any momentum, it's also a true statement that comes from my heart—a chance to remind my child how much I treasure her.

I'm not suggesting that you stop defending your positions when they are truly important, or that you allow anyone to walk over, or take advantage of, you. In fact, I think you'll agree that allowing someone else to win an argument, at least once in a while, is actually a sign of strength. It demonstrates that you are a person who can keep your bearings and sense of perspective. Not always, but usually, this opens the door for the other person to do the same.

39.

KEEP A SANE PACE

Today, more than ever, many of us live at a pace that can only be described as "crazy." In addition to the incredible demands of simply getting by, earning a living, raising a family, and attending to our daily responsibilities, many of us also attempt to partake in social, fitness, charitable or volunteer, and recreational activities as well. We are trying desperately to stay fit and be good parents, citizens, and friends. If at all possible, most of us would also like to have some fun. The problem is, each of us has only twenty-four hours in a day. There is only so much we can do.

There are many contributing factors to this increased pace of life, including technology and higher expectations. Computers, electronics, and other forms of technology have made our world seem smaller and masked our limitation of time. We can do everything much more quickly than ever before. Unfortunately, this has contributed to a sense of impatience, of wanting things to happen immediately. I've seen people annoyed because they had to wait a few minutes at a fast-food restaurant, or bothered because their computers took more than a few seconds to boot up. We get stressed over a little traffic and completely lose sight of the fact that we're traveling relatively quickly in a comfortable automobile or bus. Indeed, it seems that our expectations have increased to the point that many of us want to do everything. Nothing is good enough—we have to have more and do more.

If we try to do too much, we end up frantically rushing around from one thing to the next. And when we are hurried, we are more easily bothered and have the tendency to sweat the small stuff! In addition, when we are rushed, we rarely feel a sense of satisfaction for what we are doing because we are so focused on getting to the next activity. Instead of being in the moment, we are off to the next one.

Keeping a sane pace does more than keep us sane. It brings a richness to our experience that is impossible to experience when we are rushing around too quickly. There is something magical about having a little space between activities, a sense of calm, of having enough time. I have found that keeping a sane pace is a reward in and of itself, a satisfying experience in its own right.

If I had to choose between doing five things in a hurried, rushed manner, or four things calmly and peacefully, I'd choose the latter. Obviously, there will be times when rushing around is a fact of life that you may not be able to avoid. Sometimes, it seems that you have to be in two or three places at the same time! However, there is usually some amount of rushing around that is self-created. By simply becoming aware of your own speeded-up tendency, and by having the goal of keeping a sane pace, you may find subtle ways to slow down your life and become a little calmer and stress free. I think you'll find that if you can slow down, even slightly, the quality of your life will be enhanced in many ways.

40.

DON'T BE A MARTYR

Needless to say, we all make many sacrifices and trade-offs in our relationships and family lives. Most of these sacrifices are well worth it. But, as with most things (including good things), too much is still too much.

Obviously, the tolerance levels to stress, responsibility, lack of sleep, sacrifice, hardship, and everything else are going to vary from person to person. In other words, something that's supereasy for you might be quite difficult for me—and vice versa. However, if we can pay attention to, and be honest about, our feelings, each of us knows when the level of stress has risen too high. When it does, we usually feel incredibly frustrated, agitated, and perhaps most of all, resentful. We may feel a little self-righteous and convince ourselves that we're working harder than other people and that we have it tougher than everyone else.

Many of us (myself included) have fallen prey to the seduction of becoming a martyr. It's easy to have this happen because there is often a fine line between working hard out of actual necessity and overdoing it out of perceived necessity.

The sad truth is, however, that no one actually benefits from or appreciates a martyr. To himself, a martyr is his own worst enemy—constantly filling his head with lists of things to do and always reminding himself how difficult his life is. This mental ambush saps the joy from his life. And to the people around him, a martyr is an overly serious complainer who is too self-absorbed to see the beauty of life. Rather than feeling sorry for him, or seeing him as a victim, as the martyr would love to see happen, outsiders usually see a martyr's problems as being completely self-created.

If you think you may have martyr tendencies, I urge you to give them up! Rather than spending 100 percent of your energy doing things for other people, leave something for someone else to do. Take up a hobby. Spend a few minutes a day doing something just for you—something you really enjoy. You'll be amazed by two things. First, you'll actually start to enjoy your life and experience more energy as you feel less stressed. Nothing takes more energy than feeling resentful and victimized. Second, as you let go of resentment and the feeling that everything you do you do out of obligation, the others around you will begin to appreciate you more than before. Rather than feeling as if you resent them, they will feel as if you enjoy and appreciate them instead—which you will. In short, everyone wins and benefits when you give up your victim attitude and your tendency to be a martyr.

41.

LET GO OF YOUR EXPECTATIONS

If ever there was a suggestion that was easier said than done, this would be it. Expectations are a part of life and seem to be ingrained into our thinking. However, if you can lessen your expectations (even a little bit) about how things are supposed to be, and instead open your heart and acceptance to what is, you'll be well on your way to a calmer and much happier life.

The truth is, our expectations are responsible for a great deal of our grief and stress. We expect something to be a certain way or a person to behave in a certain way and it doesn't happen—so we get upset, bothered, disappointed, and unhappy. Since life is rarely exactly the way we would like it to be, or the way we expect it should be, we end up spending a great deal of time let down or disappointed, constantly wishing life were different than it actually is. Then, rather than seeing our own part in the process, we continue to blame life and our circumstances for our stress and frustration.

Just yesterday, Kris caught me in this psychological trap. I tend to be a very enthusiastic person, and one of my buttons is when other people (especially my family) fail to meet my expectation that they should also be enthusiastic. In this particular instance, it was a really hot day and I was excited about going to the community pool where we are members. But when I asked the kids if they wanted to go along with me, their response was less than I had hoped for. Instead of "Great idea, Dad, we can't wait," it was a little more like "Yeah, whatever." Their response sent me into a tailspin as I blurted out the question, "What's wrong with everyone around here?" It probably would have gotten worse, but Kris jumped in with a smile and said, "What was that you were saying about opening your heart to 'what is' instead of insisting on it being a certain way?" Enough said!

In no way am I suggesting that you eliminate your preferences or all of your expectations. Certainly there will be times when you will want to insist on certain things or demand certain standards of behavior, and that's fine. But lessening your expectations is *not* the same thing as lowering your standards! It's entirely possible to have very high standards, yet still keep your perspective about your own expectations. Keep in mind that our goal here is to improve the quality of our lives and to keep the little things from taking over our lives. It's ultimately in your best interest if you can see the importance of letting go of some of your expectations. That way, you can enjoy more of your life the way it really is and struggle less with the way you would rather it be.

42.

APPRECIATE YOUR IN-LAWS

Admittedly, this has been an easy one for me because my in-laws, Pat and Ted, are extraordinary people. And I must say that my wife is equally lucky because my parents are also quite special. However, for many people, in-laws present quite a personal challenge, to say the least. And even if you like your in-laws, you do have to make certain sacrifices simply because of the nature of marriage. You will, for example, have to make trade-offs as to where you spend holidays. You will also have to deal with the almost unavoidable problems of conflicting backgrounds and upbringings—different religious philosophies, differing views on parenting, discipline, spending, saving, the relative importance of spending time with family, and so forth. Yet, despite the probable differences among you, I believe that most in-law relationships have the potential to be loving and filled with mutual respect.

The trick to making the most of your relationship with your in-laws is to stay focused on gratitude. While there almost certainly will be differences you will have to deal with, gratitude will enable you to appreciate, rather than struggle against, those differences.

It's easy to forget, yet if you love your spouse, you owe your in-laws an enormous debt of gratitude! If not for their bringing your spouse into the world, you would be with someone else, or alone. In most instances, it took your in-laws (or one of them) to raise your spouse. So, regardless of what you may think, they played a significant role in your spouse's upbringing.

Before you sarcastically think something like "That explains why my spouse has certain problems," keep in mind that the opposite is equally true. If you blame your in-laws for any issues your spouse struggles with, it's only fair to give them credit for his or her strengths as well. In addition, if you have children, their genes—their physical makeup—come, in part, from your in-laws. Without their contribution, your children would not be the people they are. If you think your kids are cute, and who doesn't think so, some of that cuteness, whether you want to believe it or not, comes from your in-laws.

Believe me, I'm not a bury-your-head-in-the-sand-and-pretend-that-everything-is-perfect kind of person. I realize that all in-laws have certain difficult qualities, just as I will to my future son-in-law, some-day down the road (way down the road). However, what choice do you have? You can continue to complain about your in-laws, make mean-spirited jokes about how difficult it is to have them, and wish that they were different—or you can begin to focus less on their irritating quirks and characteristics and instead focus on that which you have to be grateful for. I believe the decision is an easy one. Stay focused on gratitude and my guess is that you'll be able to improve your existing relationship in a significant way.

43.

MOODS AND HOME LIFE

Moods are one of those unavoidable, mysterious, and sometimes annoying facts of life that everyone must deal with. However, an understanding of moods can help you deflect a large
percentage of would-be annoyances, making your life seem smoother
and more manageable.

Moods are like "internal weather," constantly changing. And with
our changing moods come different perceptions of life. Generally
speaking, when you are in a good mood, or a nice state of mind, life
looks pretty darn good. Despite the imperfections, you feel grateful for
your family and for your home. For the most part, you accept your life
for what it is and make an effort to make the best of it. Problems don't
seem like the end of the world and solutions seem to present themselves with relative ease. You feel lucky to have a family and a home to
live in. If you have a garden, you are in awe of its beauty. In high
moods, you adore your children and your spouse. You're proud of the
way you work together and how much love is expressed in your home.
You take your responsibilities in stride and overlook the day-to-day
irritations that must be dealt with. If something breaks, you either fix
it or let it go. If someone criticizes you, you chuckle at yourself, know-

ing that your accuser probably has a legitimate point. In a nutshell, you maintain your perspective and sense of humor and make the best of the incredible gift of life!

In low moods, however, the *exact* same life and the *identical* circumstances look drastically different. Everything seems serious and urgent. You have very little patience or tolerance for imperfection. Instead of being grateful for your life, you tend to complain and think about its many imperfections. Although you love your children immensely, you are easily annoyed and bothered by all the attention they require and the inconvenience of taking care of their numerous needs. Your home seems more like a burden than it does a blessing. You notice and think about your spouse's imperfections and blame him or her for the problems around the home. When something spills or breaks, you turn it into front-page news on the home front. Everything seems like a big deal and a burden. In short, you sweat the small stuff in a very big way!

Relax. To one degree or another, we're all like this, sort of like Dr. Jekyll and Mr. Hyde. In a way, our mood is the source of our experience, not the effect. Our mood determines the way we see and experience our lives. As our mood goes up, our lives look better. As it drops, life seems worse, far more difficult. Again, to reinforce how significant your moods are, keep in mind how different your life looks, even from one hour to the next, depending on what kind of mood you are in.

Simple as it sounds, learning to detect what mood you are in and make allowances for changing moods can make an enormous difference in the quality of your life and can tone down your reactivity in a very significant way. The important thing is to accept the fact that changing moods are a fact of life and to understand the absolute inevitability of the way you are going to experience your lower moods. Remember, it's not your life that has suddenly changed for the worse in the past hour, it's your mood.

Recognizing this can give you a great deal of perspective. You can learn to expect to see things in a negative light when you are feeling down. This expectation allows you to take less seriously whatever it is that is bugging you. You can learn to blame your mood instead of your life and your family for your troubles. Keep in mind that if something were truly responsible for your negative feelings, it would bother you all the time. However, virtually nothing falls into this category. The truth is, a vast majority of the things that bug you in a low mood are things you are able to take in stride in a higher state of mind.

44.

SEPARATE WORK FROM

EVERYTHING ELSE

Like millions of people, and despite having an office outside the home, I also work a great deal at home. In fact, I'm writing this sentence in my upstairs office before the sun has started to rise.

There are few things more predictable than the stress you create for yourself when you fail to separate your work from the rest of your life. I don't mean you shouldn't work at home, only that you should take steps toward separating your work from the rest of your life.

If you're going to work at home, if at all possible have a separate phone line and a room that is dedicated solely to your work. I've heard many people say, "It's not worth the extra expense to have a separate phone line." What these people aren't taking into consideration is the fact that many people are annoyed by businesses whose phones are answered by someone *other* than the person associated with the business. For example, despite being a pretty easygoing person, I have to admit that I find it a little disconcerting when I'm trying to reach someone (on whom I'm going to spend money) and a child answers the phone, or a spouse who has little or no knowledge of what's going on. I often wonder if the person I'm trying to reach is really going to get my message! Sometimes, it's just easier to find someone else who makes the effort to make my experience (as the customer) an easier one. It's very possible that you could actually lose customers or future referrals by mixing your personal phone line with that of your business. In most cases, one lost customer is going to cost far more than a monthly service charge from your phone company.

But beyond your phone, there's the "organization factor." The more you are able to keep your work separated from your home life, the less often you'll lose or misplace things. You'll know where to find your date book, your projects, phone numbers, and other important information. Things won't be so likely to get mixed up. You'll think of your work space as just that—your work space. And your home will be yours to enjoy. You'll feel more organized and less stressed out.

When you combine your work space with your living space—when you share a phone, carry papers around the house, work in different rooms—you'll be far more inclined to make social calls and do other, nonwork-related, activities than you would if you kept everything separate. The reason for this is obvious—you're used to calling your friends in the living room, or tidying up while you're in the kitchen. By keeping everything separate, however, you'll be far more productive and waste less time.

I have learned to keep my work separate from everything else. My kids aren't allowed to play on my laptop computer, nor are they allowed to play with my files or use my fax machine. The result of my conscious effort to keep everything separate is that I'm not only more productive but, in addition, I'm substantially less stressed out than I used to be when I allowed my home and work lives to be one and the same. My guess is that, if you give this strategy a try, you'll be far less inclined to sweat the small stuff at home because you'll be less nervous about the consequences of mixing your work with the rest of your life. Now that I've finished writing this section, I think I'll go downstairs and see what the kids are doing!

45.

WORK ON ABSOLUTE ACCEPTANCE

OF THOSE YOU LOVE MOST

It's sad, but in many cases the people we love unconditionally the *least* are the people we love the *most*. In other words, while we can quite easily overlook or simply ignore the negativity or idiosyncrasies of complete strangers, it's difficult to do the same with our children or our spouses.

This was brought to my attention by a dear friend of mine who noticed my very high expectations of my two daughters. She said to me, "It seems to me that in many areas of your parenting you are quite accepting, but are you aware that, to a large degree, you seem to expect your children to always be enthusiastic and happy?" She went on to ask, "Can you imagine how difficult that expectation would be to live up to?" It was like a whack on the side of my head! Her observation hurt a little, but boy was it right on. It has turned out to be an important insight that has helped me a great deal.

My friend was absolutely right. For the most part, I'm perfectly okay with the fact that most people aren't always happy. I believe I do an excellent job at accepting people exactly as they are. However, I had developed the habit of acting very disappointed in my own children virtually anytime they expressed any emotion other than happiness.

What I learned was that I, like most people, levy my most demanding expectations on those people whom I love the most. Think about some of the obvious examples: If a neighbor spilled a glass of milk on the floor, you'd probably say "Oh, don't worry about it, I'll clean it up," but if your child did the exact same thing, would you act the same? Or might you act disappointed, angry, or frustrated? Yet, your child is the one you love with all your heart—not your neighbor. Or you might be very accepting of the "innocent" little quirks of a family friend but feel as if you're going to be driven crazy by your spouse's quirks, even though they are very similar.

I don't want to get overly analytical here about the reasons for this twisted set of values. I believe what's most important is that we recognize our own tendency to have extremely high expectations for our loved ones and that we set out to love more unconditionally. In my case, what was most helpful was to practice remembering that people are different in the ways they express themselves—including my own children. I needed to respect my children and their ways of being in the same way that I have always tried to respect everyone else. And you know what, it really works! I believe my children have sensed my sincere desire to become less judgmental and more unconditionally loving. And I have felt a similar love coming from each of them. If you make it a top priority to accept those whom you love the most, I think you'll be richly rewarded by the love you'll feel in your family.

46.

DON'T SWEAT THE LITTLE QUIRKS

In some ways, it's no wonder that the people you live with can drive you crazy with their little quirks. You know, the way someone eats, uses utensils, breathes, flits her hair, jiggles his leg, stacks pennies, stomps his or her feet, or whatever. After all, chances are you spend more time with these people than with anyone else. Therefore, you have far more opportunities to experience and become familiar with the quirks and idiosyncrasies of your family members than you do with anyone else. Over time, you come to expect, even anticipate, these quirks, and when they occur they tend to annoy you.

Let's face it. There isn't a person alive who doesn't have his or her share of irritating quirks. I have so many I'd be embarrassed to share them with you. And if you were really honest, I'll bet you'd admit to having a few of your own. But despite these innocent quirks, I'll bet you're a really nice person with many fine qualities. I'd like to think I fall into the same category.

The point is, we're all human. Whether you live alone and only have to deal with your *own* little quirks (or those of any pets you might have), or whether you have a spouse and a bunch of kids and have dozens of quirks to contend with on a regular basis, we're all in this together. To be human is to have quirks. Big deal!

Many people are easily bothered by their own quirks and by those of their family members. They focus on them and wish they would go away. They share their displeasure with their closest friends. But guess what? The chances of those pesky quirks' going away are about as good as my chances of winning the Wimbledon tennis championship—zero, none. Okay, maybe once in a great while someone will outgrow an annoying quirk and/or change a pattern or habit. But this is extremely rare and, in most cases, highly unlikely. Think about it. Doesn't the friend in whom you are confiding regarding your spouse's irritating quirks have a few of his or her own? What's more, do you think your friend might, on occasion, discuss *your* little imperfections with his or her other friends?

You really have only two options when it comes to dealing with quirks. You can continue to be critical of, and be bothered by, the little quirks that exist in your household. Or you can choose to see the innocence and humor that is inherent in virtually all quirks. After all, no one wants annoying quirks to be part of his or her personal makeup—we certainly don't set out to create them! They develop unintentionally and continue out of pure habit. In addition, it's important to keep in mind that, if you were to live with someone else, he or she too would quickly exhibit a variety of quirks. And who knows? They might be even more annoying than the ones you are currently forced to deal with.

Why not make the decision to make those little quirks a little less relevant? Doing so is a huge relief. You will no longer have to spend mental energy reminding yourself how irritated you are—therefore feeling the effects of that irritation. And you'll find that when you're more forgiving and accepting of everyone else, it's far easier to be easier on yourself. So, starting today, whatever "small stuff" around the house bugs you, see if you can let it go! You'll be so much happier as a result.

47.

WHEN SOMEONE ASKS YOU HOW YOU ARE, DON'T EMPHASIZE HOW BUSY YOU ARE

Putting too much emphasis on our busyness has become a way of life, almost a knee-jerk reaction. In fact, I'd guess that one of the most common responses to the greeting "How are you doing?" has become "I'm so busy." As I write about this strategy, I have to admit that, at times, I'm as guilty of this tendency as anyone else. However, I've noticed that as I've become more conscious of it, I'm putting less and less emphasis on my own busyness—and I'm feeling a whole lot better as a result.

It's almost as though we become more comfortable after confirming to others that, we too, are very busy. I was in the grocery story last night on my way home from work when I witnessed two sets of friends greeting one another. The first person said, "Hi, Chuck. How's it going?" Chuck sighed loudly and said, "Really busy, how about you?" His friend responded, "Yeah, me too. I've been working really hard."

Then, almost as if the customers in the store knew I was writing a book, two women added to my material! Not more than a few seconds later, out of the corner of my eye, I heard one woman say to the other, "Grace, nice to see you. How's everything?" Grace's response was to noticeably shrug her shoulders and say, "Pretty good, but really busy," followed by a polite and seemingly sincere "How about you?" The answer: "You know, busy as ever."

It's very tempting to enter into a conversation with these words because the truth is that most of us *are* really busy. Also, many people feel they have to be busy or they have no value in our society. Some people are even competitive about how busy they are. The problem, however, is that this response and overemphasis on how busy we are sets the tone for the rest of the conversation. It puts the emphasis on busyness by reminding both parties how stressful and complicated life has become. So, despite the fact that you have a moment to escape your stressful existence by saying hello to a friend or acquaintance, you are choosing to spend even your spare moments emphasizing and reminding yourself how busy you are.

Despite the fact that this response may have elements of honesty, it works against you—and your friend—by reinforcing your feelings of busyness. True, you're busy, but that's not all you are! You're also an interesting person with many other qualities besides busyness. The fact that most of us emphasize how busy we are to others isn't entirely necessary but is simply a habit many of us have fallen into. We can change this habit by simply recognizing that it exists—and exploring other options.

I think you'll be amazed at how much more relaxed you'll become if you do nothing more than change your initial comments to people you see or talk to on the phone. As an experiment, try to eliminate any discussion about how busy you are for an entire week! It may be difficult, but it will be worth it. You'll notice that, despite being as busy as ever, you'll begin to *feel* slightly less busy. You'll also notice that, as you deemphasize how busy you are, the people you speak to will sense permission from you to place a little less emphasis on their own busyness, helping them to feel a little less stressed and perhaps encouraging your entire conversation to be more nourishing and jointly relaxing. So, the next time someone asks you how you are doing, say anything *except* "I'm really busy." You'll be glad you did.

48.

GIVE YOUR NEIGHBORS A BREAK

It's easy to let your neighbors get on your nerves. After all, most of us live next to, or at least very close to, other people. We hear our neighbors through the walls or over the fence, see them often, and have the opportunity to witness some of their most annoying habits. We must deal with their pets, their messes, their garbage cans, and their voices. Sometimes we must look at their messy yards or their unkempt lawns. We are forced to look at their unfinished home projects, their weeds, and their half-painted fences. Sometimes we even hear their arguments and other things they might not want us to hear. Is it any wonder there are so many neighbors who can't seem to get along? If you sweat the small stuff with your neighbors, you might very well feel like you're going to go crazy, because there will always be lots of small stuff to contend with!

The best solution for keeping your sanity is to keep in mind something you might not want to hear or admit. However, it's important to remember that it's equally tough on our neighbors—they have to deal with us! I can assure you that, from their perspective, we're equally, or perhaps even more, difficult to deal with than they are.

If you're set on being right and insisting that your neighbors are difficult, while you are the perfect neighbor, it's going to be difficult to convince you otherwise. However, if you can imagine reversing roles with your neighbor, if just for a few minutes, and trying to see things from their perspective, it might help you relax just a little.

Often, when people rent an apartment or buy a home, they feel (quite justifiably so) that they have sacrificed long and hard and deserve to live the way they choose. If you're honest, you may feel this way too. The last thing most people want is a neighbor trying to tell them how their yard should look, demanding that their dog be quiet or that they keep their voices down after ten o'clock.

It's important to put yourself in your neighbors' shoes. Try to have compassion for their perspective. This doesn't mean you need to roll over and allow them to abuse you in any way—or that your demands aren't reasonable and that you shouldn't do what you can to change truly important things. It does suggest, however, that you should choose your battles very carefully. You can learn to disagree on the standards of your neighborhood without unnecessary ruffles in your feathers. You can learn to deal with your neighbors in a nondefensive manner without being bothered or upset. And when you do, you'll discover that a vast majority of neighbors are a lot like you. Most people truly do want to live in peace and with mutual respect. The problem is, many people have had negative experiences with neighbors and approach the relationship, and all related conflicts, in a defensive way. What this means, in reality, is that they are looking for reasons to distrust or disagree with you. They have their guard up; they are defensive, ready for battle. If you give them any evidence to support their assumptions, they will quickly turn difficult and demanding.

If this is true with you and/or your neighbors, the best you can do is to try to bring out the best in your neighbors rather than the worst. Open your heart and try to get a fresh start. See if there are things you can do to improve your relationship. Be the first one to reach out and seek peace. Invite your neighbor over for coffee. Ask yourself questions like "What can I do to make this relationship a little better?" and "What have I done to contribute to our problems?" You can't change your neighbor, but you can change your own reactions.

Another way you can give your neighbors a break is to try to focus not on their annoying habits but on the things they do right. It's easy, for example, to focus on an occasional late-night party hosted by your neighbor's teenager but to totally forget that 95 percent of the time those same neighbors are completely silent. This is a good time to avoid sweating the small stuff. It's usually pretty easy to sleep in a different room or to put earplugs in during the party if you're having trouble sleeping through the noise. And if you're honest, it probably takes you ten minutes to clean up any mess in your yard. In all likelihood, there's a party a few times a year. By giving your neighbors a break, they will think of you in a much kinder light. They will be far more considerate and more tolerant of your annoying habits. If you give your neighbors a break, I think you'll find that living in harmony is much easier than you imagined it to be.

49.

ACKNOWLEDGE THE UNIQUE
HARDSHIPS OF YOUR
FAMILY MEMBERS

We all know that life can, at times, be overwhelming. However, it's much easier to spot and acknowledge our own sources of feeling overwhelmed than it is to see the problems of the others in our family. For example, if you work outside the home and your spouse (husband or wife) is at home, it may be tempting to focus on, and discuss, the difficulties of *your* day but remain somewhat indifferent or oblivious to the difficulties of your spouse. Or the reverse may be true. You may be absorbed in how difficult it is to be at home with the kids but lose sight of the fact that it's also stressful and difficult to work away from the house all day long. It's even easier to forget that children and teens have their own struggles that are very real to them. The fact that it's difficult to understand why life seems so challenging to our younger family members doesn't mean that those problems aren't real—they are.

How often have you heard the expression "He/she just doesn't understand me?" This statement is extremely common when wives and husbands discuss their spouses with friends. It's even more common when kids are discussing their parents with their friends. Sadly, many family members feel all alone, as if no one within their family truly understands them.

This is a relatively easy problem to overcome. The solution is to become more compassionate and to try to put yourself in the shoes of your family members—your husband, wife, kids, parents, or siblings. Try to imagine what it's like to be your husband, wife, child, or other family member. See if you can understand the unique challenges they face. Imagine how difficult it would be to be in their shoes. I have found that in all cases you'll find that their lives are not quite as easy as they may appear on the surface.

I'm not suggesting you start commiserating with your family members or that you put an overemphasis on the problems in your family. Rather, I'm suggesting that you become a better listener and more compassionate to those you love. Doing so will reduce your own stress levels by reminding you that you're not alone in your struggles. It will also assist everyone in your family in reducing their stress levels as well. The simple act of genuine and caring acknowledgment is a source of healing and comfort, particularly when it comes from someone you love.

One of the surest ingredients of bringing two family members closer together is the feeling of being understood and listened to. Rather than focusing on your own challenges and burdens, try to be more compassionate to the issues of the others. You'll be amazed at how quickly your feelings of closeness will return and how much less frequently you'll be sweating the small stuff.

50.

DON'T GO TO BED MAD

I learned this bit of wisdom from my parents, and I've appreciated it my entire life. While I was growing up, this family philosophy cut short, or nipped in the bud, many arguments, angry evenings, and negative feelings that would have undoubtedly carried forward to the next day, or perhaps even longer. The idea is that, despite the fact that all families have their share of problems and issues to contend with, nothing is so bad that it's worth going to bed mad over. What this strategy ensures is that, regardless of what's happening, who's to blame, or how mad you or someone else in your family happens to be, there is a set cap or limit to your anger, at which time everyone in the family agrees it's time to let go, forgive, apologize, and start over. No exceptions. This limit is bedtime.

When you have an absolute policy that no one goes to bed mad, it helps you remember that love and forgiveness are never far away. It encourages you to bend a little, to be the first to reach out and open the dialogue, offer a genuine hug, and keep your heart open. When you make the decision to never go to bed mad, it helps you see the innocence in your own behavior and in that of your family members. It keeps the channels of communication open. It reminds you that you are a family and that, despite your problems and disagreements, you love, need, and treasure each other. The decision that it's never a good idea to go to bed mad is a built-in reset button that protects your family from stress, hostility, and resentment.

Perhaps it's easier to see the importance of such a policy in its absence. Without a family policy such as this, arguments and anger are open-ended. No one will have created a boundary, a set of rules that protect your family from extended and unnecessary anger. Without a rule to suggest otherwise, family members can hold on to their anger and justify doing so.

Kris and I have tried very hard to implement this strategy in our family. While it's not perfect, and while occasionally one or more of us seems a little frustrated at bedtime, on balance it's been enormously helpful. It ensures that ninety-nine times out of one hundred, we'll wake up the next morning with love in our hearts and with an attitude of "This is a new day." I hope that you'll give this strategy a fair try. It's certainly not always easy, and you probably won't bat 100 percent, but it's well worth the effort. Remember, life is short. Nothing is so important that it's worth ruining your day, nor is anything so significant that it's worth going to bed mad. Have a nice sleep.

51.

ASK YOURSELF "WHY SHOULD I BE EXEMPT FROM THE REST OF THE HUMAN RACE?"

A number of years ago I was complaining to a friend of mine about how much responsibility I had and how difficult my life seemed to be. His response played a role in my transformation from seeing myself as a victim of circumstance to being a person who truly accepts life as it is (most of the time). Rather than commiserating with me and sharing his own difficulties, his question to me was, "Is there some reason why you think you should be exempt from the rest of the human race?"

He was referring, of course, to the obvious, but largely overlooked, fact that life is full of challenges, obstacles, hurdles, setbacks, difficulties, hassles, and problems—for all of us. No one is exempt. Regardless of your background, race, religion, or sex—regardless of what kind of parents you had, your birth order, how much money or notoriety you have, and all the other specifics of your life—you will have problems. Case closed.

It's always easier to see your own problems than those of others, and it's certainly true that some problems appear to be far more severe than others, but the truth is, ultimately no one's life is particularly easy, at least not all of the time. The old saying is still true, as it will be forever: Circumstances don't make a person, they reveal him or her.

It's very helpful to remind yourself of this fact of life. It puts things in perspective. When we remind ourselves that life wasn't meant to be hassle-free or perfect, we are more able to respond to our challenges with perspective and grace. Rather than being annoyed or overwhelmed by every little thing, we're usually able to say something like "Oh, well, here's another one to deal with."

I doubt very much that any of us will get to the point where we enjoy the inherent hassles of life, but I'm certain that we can learn to be far more accepting. And, as you can imagine, the less you struggle with your problems and challenges, the more energy you have at your disposal to solve them. Rather than exacerbating the issues you are dealing with, you'll see the bigger picture, including the best possible solutions at hand.

Reminding yourself of the inevitability of problems to deal with won't make your life perfect, but it will put things in a healthier perspective and make life seem a whole lot less overwhelming. Starting right now, see if you can view your current problems in a new light. You might discover that at least the "small stuff" can be experienced with a great deal more serenity.

52.

LET YOURSELF OFF THE HOOK

My dear wife, Kris, saved me one day with this comforting suggestion. I had been working very hard, traveling quite a bit on business, and was dreadfully behind on several of my projects. I had let my schedule get a little out of control and I hadn't had a minute to myself in several weeks. I was at least a week behind on returning phone calls and had missed several important social engagements, as well as two very significant events that my daughters were involved in. I was feeling overwhelmed and as though everyone was mad at me. At the same time, my office looked extremely disorganized, and since I had been too busy to exercise, I felt like I was getting out of shape.

That's when Kris (bless her heart) gave me a hug and said, "Richard, let yourself off the hook." She reminded me that I didn't have to be perfect and that it wasn't possible to be all things to all people all the time (or any of the time). I had clearly drifted off balance, and it was time to regain my bearings.

Kris's point is an important one for so many of us. Often, we try to do everything. We work hard, stay organized, try our best to be good parents, spouses, friends, and concerned citizens. At the same time, we try to squeeze some exercise into the mix, and pay our taxes!

We bake, clean our homes (constantly), walk the dog, and take care of the garden. In addition, some of us volunteer our time and even try to do some reading.

Sometimes, it's all too much to handle. This is the time to let yourself off the hook. Remind yourself that you don't have to be perfect or put yourself on a pedestal! If you've been really busy and don't have time to get the house cleaned, see if you can put it off until a little later. If three friends called in the same day asking you to return their calls and you feel tired or too overwhelmed, see if you can wait a day to respond, or at least call them and be honest about how you are feeling and see if you can postpone the conversation. Or, if you mess up and forget an appointment, rather than berate yourself for how stupid you are, see if you can use the mistake as a signal that you probably have too much on your plate.

In this day and age when so many of us are trying to be perfect, or act like we are superpeople, it's tremendously helpful to let yourself off the hook. As simple as it sounds, reminding yourself that you don't have to be perfect is an excellent way to lighten up and take some pressure off yourself.

In my example above, when I was able to give myself a break in this manner, my life seemed to come back together very quickly. As I began to relax, my kids and friends offered me more compassion and my work life began to mellow a bit. Within a relatively short period of time, my life was back to normal. In fact, it was better than normal! From time to time I still need to remind myself of the same thing, but each time I do, I rediscover the beauty of this simple message.

53.

REMEMBER, ACTIONS SPEAK

LOUDER THAN WORDS

I believe this bit of wisdom is always important to keep in mind, but never more so than at home. Yet, as often as most of us have heard it, how many of us live our lives as if we knew that it were true?

One of my many favorite quotes is from Ralph Waldo Emerson. He said, "What you do speaks so loud that I cannot hear what you say." This quote has come in handy as Kris and I attempt to raise our kids. It reminds us that what we say may be important, but not nearly as important as what we do.

One of the most obvious places where this wisdom takes form is our decision as to how we spend our time. It's easy to say to your children or your spouse, for example, "You are the most important part of my life." However, to a child (and most likely a spouse too), actions really do speak louder than words. If you spend twelve hours a day at the office and five or ten minutes with the "most important people" in your life, there is an enormous inconsistency between your words and your actions. There are more subtle forms of the same dynamic, as well. For example, if the telephone always takes precedence over spending time with a child, the message received is: Priority #1, telephone; priority #2, me! Or, if there's always something that must be done—cooking, dishes, cleaning up, unreturned calls—before time with the family, the message is equally clear.

I understand that life isn't perfect, and I know you do too. There are trade-offs all of us must make, and it's difficult to keep an appropriate balance. Virtually everyone must work to earn a living, and sometimes work takes up most of your waking time. Often, there's not a darn thing you can do about it.

Despite all this, however, there are things we *can* do. There are countless little ways we can show our families and loved ones that they really are our #1 priority. We can turn down opportunities—business related or personal—and choose instead to spend time with those we truly love. The most important thing to understand, however, isn't the choice itself but the attitude we carry with the choice. We need to make it clear that we are making our choice happily and joyfully. Rather than feeling like victims because we get very little time for ourselves, we can make it crystal clear that we are truly blessed to be with our loved ones. I recently turned down an enormous speaking opportunity because what I really wanted to do was be at my daughter's soccer game. I tried to make it clear, however, that this wasn't a sacrifice. I was the lucky one. And I was richly rewarded. She scored her very first goal—ever!

There are other, more subtle, ways you can accomplish the same goal. I know there are exceptions, but you must admit that there are times we stay late at the office by choice instead of by necessity. Are you doing something truly relevant, or are you doing something more optional, something that can wait? Is it as important as time with your family?

If you're talking to your spouse or child and the phone rings, you can avoid jumping up and answering it. Instead, you can remain interested in your present conversation—you can stay right where you are. You might even say to your family member, "There is no one I'd rather talk to than you." If you're genuine, you won't believe how much this simple sentence can mean to someone you love.

Additionally, you can become more patient and a better listener, really focusing on what your family members are saying rather than waiting for your turn to interrupt or your chance to run away to the next important thing you have to do. It all adds up. Every positive choice that you make reinforces the love in your family and decreases any resentment, disappointment, or sadness that might have developed over time.

If you want loving, mutually respectful relationships at home, your decisions don't have to be monumental, but they do have to make it clear that, on balance, your family really is the most important part of your life. There are hundreds of things you can do, little daily choices you can make. The specific choices you make are up to you. My goal here is simply to remind you that you are the choice maker. With a little reflection, I'll bet you can make at least one loving choice today that can make a world of difference in the quality of your life at home.

54.

LEARN TO STAY CENTERED

Regardless of your specific concerns, or what issues you are currently being confronted with, learning to stay centered is bound to help you. Being centered is a quality that brings harmony, equanimity, and balance into your life. A person who is centered is able to remain calm in the midst of crisis and is able to make wise, appropriate decisions on an ongoing basis. Being centered also keeps you from being bothered or annoyed by little things and assists you in keeping your cool. As the name suggests, being centered keeps you from being thrown off balance by the events and circumstances in your life. Being more centered will help you deal with your family, your budget, your home, and all your important decisions.

The easiest way to learn to be more centered is to keep your attention in the present moment as much as possible. By paying attention to your own thinking, you can learn to detect when the focus of your attention is too much in the past, or off somewhere in the future. Generally speaking, if you are feeling stressed, your mind will be in one of two places—in the past or in the future. And if you observe how you feel when your mind is somewhere other than the here and now, you'll notice how stressed you will feel and how easily things can bother you.

For example, if you're thinking about how busy you are and how many more things you still have to do today, and someone asks you a simple question, it can seem like a burden to offer a thoughtful response. Your focus on your own business suggests that your attention is elsewhere. It magnifies your workload and makes everything seem more difficult and demanding.

However, if your attention is more in the moment, it encourages you to do one thing at a time, as it arises. Instead of focusing on the ten things you still have to do today with scattered attention, you will learn to focus on the one thing that you are actually doing—and then the next—offering whatever it is you are doing your undivided attention. This increased focus allows you to become more efficient, and as it does, your life will begin to seem far less stressful. When you live your life moment to moment, giving each moment and event your full attention, life rarely seems overwhelming. This is because you will be less burdened and distracted by the events of your past as well as the events that will occur at some future date.

If you are centered and someone asks you a question in the midst of your busy day, you'll be far more likely to simply shift gears easily, without distress, and offer a response. Rather than being frantic a great deal of the time, you'll be far more relaxed and at ease.

Being centered brings with it a feeling of calm and ease. When you can maintain a sense of well-being, even in the midst of chaos, you'll discover that life is much easier to deal with and far more manageable than when your attention is scrambled and frantic. Rather than remembering the hard day you had yesterday, or anticipating the difficult day you are likely to have tomorrow, you'll be more able to make today the best it can possibly be.

55.

BECOME LESS EASILY BOTHERED

I was speaking at a bookstore to a crowd of people when someone asked me an interesting question: "How would you describe the average person in two words or less?" After reflecting for a
moment, I answered, "Easily bothered." The entire room burst into
laughter because everyone recognized that I had hit on an almost universal truth—most of us are bothered by practically everything.

The payback for becoming less easily bothered is monumental!
Your stress level will be reduced. You'll be more accepting of the people
and events in your life. You'll have far more fun and will become more
interested in, and interesting to, other people. You'll be a better role
model to your family and friends. You'll be less reactive. You'll see life
less as a burden and more as an adventure. You'll be less tired and
irritated. You'll turn your ordinary life into an extraordinary experience. The truth is, being bothered is no fun. It's a huge distraction to
a quality life and the ultimate expression of sweating the small stuff.
Plus, it's a real turnoff to other people.

The way to become less easily bothered is to make it a priority.
Observe your own reactions to life. Take note of how uptight you can
be and how reactive you are to the events and people around you.

When you have done so, make a commitment to becoming less bothered, especially by little things.

As you move through your day, see if you can catch yourself being annoyed or bothered. Make a game out of it. As you find yourself getting uptight over some little thing, say something to yourself like "Whoops, there I go again." Make light of it. You'll notice that most of your (over)reactions are unconscious, meaning you probably aren't even aware of how uptight you have become. By consciously paying attention to your own thinking and reactions, you bring them to the surface and enable yourself to make a change.

Most of our reactions to life are nothing more than habits, learned behavior. If we practice being rigid and uptight, that's what we will become. However, the reverse is equally true. If you can combine a little humility with the ability to catch yourself and your own reactions, and you have the determination to change, you will certainly be able to do so. I've known a great number of people (I'm one of them) who used to be high-strung and easily bothered and who are now relatively relaxed and much more efficient. Give it a try. By becoming less reactive and agitated, you'll become a happier person and you'll have a lot more fun too. One more thing: Every important person in your life will notice your positive change and will appreciate it a great deal.

56.

SCHEDULE TIME FOR KINDNESS

Admittedly, when I first thought of this strategy a few years ago, I initially discounted it as being somewhat shallow. After all, I thought, if I'm a kind person, why in the world would I have to schedule time for kindness? However, I gave it a try, and much to my surprise, it has turned out to be extremely helpful in making me a kinder and more gentle person. Essentially, the idea evolved out of my observation that it's so easy to get caught up in my own little world that I can sometimes forget to slow down enough to practice the acts of kindness that I truly want to be a regular part of my life.

Obviously, the goal for many of us is to be kind all (or at least most) of the time. This strategy is not in conflict with this goal—it's a reinforcement of it. I've discovered that when I actually schedule time in my calendar for kindness, there is a natural and effortless overflow into the rest of my life. In other words, when I actually set aside time to be kind, it's easier for kindness to permeate the rest of my life.

The way this strategy works is really quite simple. You look at your calendar and set aside a little time on a regular basis—ten minutes, thirty, an hour, whatever you want—and you stick to it, like any other important scheduled appointment. During this time, you drop everything else you are doing and give this time of kindness your undivided attention.

This scheduled time for kindness is reserved for doing something (anything) thoughtful for someone else. Sometimes I use this time to write a heartfelt letter to someone I love or appreciate, write a check to charity, or make a phone call to someone for no other reason than to say "I love you." Other times, I'll reflect on ways I can contribute to society in more effective ways, or think of ways in which I might contribute in a positive way to someone else's life. Or I'll plan an event or plan to attend one—a food drive, a litter pickup, an AIDS walk, or something else. Or I'll simply close my eyes and think good thoughts for other people. What you do is absolutely up to you. There is no right or wrong way to practice this strategy. The only thing that's important here is that your intentions are loving.

This strategy has proven very powerful and effective in my life. It helps keep me centered and on track with my own stated goals. My hope is that kindness be very close to the top of my priority list, not only in my words and intentions but backed up by my actions as well. This exercise keeps me constantly reminded of this goal. It's a time for me to reflect on whether or not I'm moving in the right direction in this area of my life, and if not, it offers me an opportunity to make some simple adjustments. I think you'll be pleasantly surprised if you give this simple idea a try; it will encourage kindness and love in all aspects of your life.

57.

DON'T TALK BEHIND THEIR BACKS

I'm not at all proud of it, but I'm a person who has, from time to time, talked behind the backs of my own family members. I *am* proud, however, to report that it's becoming increasingly rare for me to do so. I've observed that, the less I fall prey to this all-too-common tendency, the more relaxed and calm I have become. In turn, I've noticed that those around me have become slightly more at ease as well. I feel better about myself because I'm no longer "gossiping," "back-stabbing," or being critical about others. And because I no longer participate in this habit, the ones I'm with are becoming less inclined to do so as well. The result has been that everyone in my immediate and extended family feels just a little better about each other. As is so often true, when a few family members break a habit, the rest of the family quickly follows suit.

When you talk behind someone's back, it says far less about the person you are discussing than it does about our own character, about your need to be critical and your need to talk behind other people's backs. It's like hitting a person who is down—the person you are talking about is not able to defend himself or herself. It's not fair.

Furthermore, if you pay careful attention to how you feel when you are critical about someone behind that person's back, you'll notice that you'll feel a little mean-spirited, as if your conscience is trying to tell you something. Deep down, you know that in most instances it's wrong to be critical of others behind their backs.

When you talk behind the backs of other people, it can also make the person you are gossiping with a little insecure. After all, if you're saying those things about someone else, what assurance do others have that you're not doing the same thing about them when they are not around? This lack of integrity greatly contributes to increased cynicism in our families and in our world because no one feels that anyone else is ultimately trustworthy.

The good news is, breaking this habit is easier than you might think. Once you see how truly nasty the habit really is, the rest seems to fall gently into place. At first, you might not notice yourself being critical until after the fact. You'll remember when it's too late. Don't be hard on yourself. Instead, be grateful that your old habit came to mind and that your goal is to stop doing it. The next time, you might catch yourself right in the middle of a conversation about someone else. You can then say something like "Whoops, there I go again being critical about someone who isn't even around." Then gently shift the conversation. At some point, it will become easy. You'll feel yourself about ready to be critical but stop short of actually doing so. You'll "see it coming," observer your own thoughts and behavior, and nip them in the bud. In time, you'll rarely be critical of others when they're not around.

Even when the people around you are talking about others, you can gently refuse to get involved. Instead, you can guide the conversation elsewhere by remaining quiet, saying something nice, or defending the person being criticized or changing the topic altogether. The benefits of being less critical behind the backs of others can be dramatic and instantaneous. Give it a try and you'll feel better right away.

58.

HAVE FAMILY MEETINGS

The purpose of family meetings is to set up a nondefensive environment in which two or more people who love each other can share freely and communicate from the heart. The idea is to create a "safe place" where everyone present is able to speak and be heard. Everyone agrees, up front, to listen very carefully to everything that is being said. No one is allowed to interrupt, attack, cut someone off, criticize, or butt in before it's his or her turn. No one is better or more important than anyone else. Everyone is treated with respect.

During a family meeting, you are allowed to share what's working for you—and what's not working. You are given permission to share honestly, without being attacked. You can tell the others about things that are bothering you and you can offer potential solutions. You can also share the parts of family life that you love the most and what would make your family even better.

Family meetings are potentially very healing. In our frenzied world, it's often difficult to find the time to sit together as a family to share and listen. Yet, this is a critical component of a loving, functional family. This is an ideal time to be together, to find out what's going on with one another, to stay acquainted, or in some cases, to get acquainted. It's a chance to learn about the other members of your family, to discover what makes them tick and what makes them happy and sad. It's often the case that people discover things about their parents, children, spouses, and siblings that they didn't know. My youngest daughter once told me during a family meeting that when I gave her a certain "look" it made her nervous. Because the purpose of our meeting was to learn from one another in a nondefensive environment, I was able to see exactly what she meant. The "look" she was referring to was one of disapproval. I had no idea I was doing it. If she had brought this up in the midst of a busy day, it's doubtful if I would have been as receptive to her words. But because the whole point of our being together was to improve our family life, I was open and receptive—and able to learn. Since that time, I've been very careful to be aware of my "looks." During our next meeting, I asked her how I was doing, and she said "Much better." She felt listened to and respected.

I remember a few of the family meetings we had when I was a child. I remember learning of some of the frustrations of my parents. This helped me to see them as people—not just my parents. It helped develop my compassion and perspective.

Family meetings are extremely helpful in venting your frustration as well as reminding you of your shared love for one another. This, in turn, keeps you from "sweating the small stuff" because you won't allow small stuff to build up into big frustrations. Instead, you'll deal with things as they come up. You'll discover solutions that work for the entire family.

Family meetings won't make your life (or your family) perfect. They will, however, keep you much closer as a family. Whether you have two people in your family or ten, I encourage you to give family meetings a try. Your rewards will be significant.

59.

REMEMBER TO SHOW YOUR

APPRECIATION

Without question, one of the primary sources of resentment in most marriages—indeed, in most family relationships—is the feeling of being taken for granted, of not feeling appreciated. Sadly, many of us are so used to being around our family members that we forget to show each other how much we appreciate one another. We take each other for granted. Kids do it to their parents and vice versa; spouses are notorious for failing to demonstrate appreciation.

I have friends and acquaintances who have very loving parents who take time and energy to take care of their young grandchildren for evenings, even entire weekends, yet I've never seen my friends show the slightest appreciation for this monumental effort. The attitude seems to be "They should want to do it. After all, they are my children's grandparents." It's easy to forget that everyone wants and needs to feel appreciated—even grandparents. It's so important and so incredibly easy to do. Not feeling appreciated is one of the major sources of burnout. I've seen a lack of appreciation destroy marriages, parent-child relationships, and sibling-sibling (as well as every other type of family) relationships.

My suggestion here is very simple. Whenever the opportunity presents itself, and whenever there is the slightest indication that it's appropriate to show your appreciation, bend over backwards to do so. Say "Thank you" often, and from your heart. Write thank-you cards and do nice things for others who do nice things for you.

Last weekend, I was privileged to deliver part of a eulogy. My wife's great-uncle Miles, whom we all loved dearly, had passed away a few days before. He meant so much to the entire family that he will be dearly missed.

Just today, Kris and I received a beautiful note from Miles's son and daughter-in-law. In part, the letter read, "Richard, Miles loved you from the first time he met you. He described you as a fine person and as the only young person who had taken the time to write a thank-you note after you first visited his lake cabin." That's the power of appreciation. Miles had remembered something as simple as a thank-you for the rest of his life. It stood out because gratitude is somewhat rare in our culture.

When someone feels appreciated, he or she is so much happier and easier to be around. If you have kids, let them know that you appreciate them. Kris and I sometimes thank our children for being a part of our family. We really mean it too! Be sure to thank everyone else in your family as well—your parents, siblings, relatives, everyone. Let them all know how much you value them. You'll be amazed at the results. Everyone loves to feel appreciated—absolutely everyone

In my experience, there is a direct relationship between families who demonstrate appreciation and families who stick together, physically and emotionally. Teenagers who feel valued and appreciated are easier to be around and learn to appreciate themselves. Wives who feel appreciated love and admire their husbands, and husbands who feel appreciated love and admire their wives. The same is true with siblings, both when sharing a home as well as when they are grown-up and on their own. I have two wonderful sisters, one older and one younger. Both are great at sharing their love and appreciation for me, and I try to do the same for them. Without question, this is one of the reasons why we remain connected and make time for each other.

60.

PUT THINGS IN PERSPECTIVE

One of the major themes of this book is that, while it's easy to allow little things to take over our lives, there are things we can do to make life around the house less stressful. I believe that one of the most important things we can do is to put things in perspective.

Of course, putting things in perspective can seem a little vague. After all, what does that really mean? I've thought a great deal about this issue, and, to me, it simply means remembering that most of the things that upset us the most are not life-or-death emergencies. In fact, I find it fascinating that when people are confronted with truly "big stuff"—natural disasters, divorce, financial crisis, illness, death of loved ones, sick children, aging parents, and so forth—most of them are remarkably courageous and innovative. For some reason, we respond to major life events by rising to the occasion, calling on our inner strength, and getting through whatever it is that life has to offer. We pray, ask for help, become highly creative, and exhibit enormous endurance.

However, the same people (all of us) who somehow get through a chemical addiction, business disaster, or some other crisis, are often overwhelmed, bent out of shape, easily annoyed, stressed out, frustrated, and bothered by all the daily "small stuff" that is part of everyone's life. Somehow, it's the little stuff, not the big stuff, that we struggle with the most.

I've found it to be very helpful to remind myself—each and every day—how trivial most things really are. Whether it's dealing with bills, crabby or demanding children, a messy home, pesky neighbors, a barking dog, an overwhelming schedule, a teenage party next door, a quarrel with my spouse, a traffic jam, an unreturned phone call, weeds in the yard, whatever—in reality, it's all small stuff. I watch the news and remind myself that the stuff I have to deal with isn't front-page news. A vast, vast majority of the time, it's not life-or-death. And if I see all the things confronting me as small stuff instead of as a series of major emergencies, it's all so much easier to deal with. With perspective, life is smoother and more manageable.

We're all so blessed to be alive, to be God's guests on this beautiful planet. Whether it takes us thirty minutes or forty-five minutes to get home from work need not interfere with our gratitude. If our kids are bickering, we can get all upset and let it ruin our day, or we can accept it as part of raising a family. If our homes aren't perfectly clean, we can feel defeated and worthless, or we can remember how fortunate we are to have a shelter to live in. If we can't afford the vacation we really want, we can feel victimized and sorry for ourselves, or we can plan a special adventure within our own budget. I could probably go on for many pages, but the point is that our response is up to us. We can complain that life isn't perfect and wait for life to accommodate us with fewer demands, or we can put things in perspective and lighten up a little. If you're like most people, you've probably already tried the struggle approach to life. My suggestion is that we all strive to become a little more accepting of life and take it as it comes, put things in perspective. The more we're able to do so, the happier and less stressed we will become.

61.

DON'T OVER EMPHASIZE
YOUR VACATIONS

Obviously, a vast majority of life is *not* spent on vacation. Yet, many of us emphasize the importance of our vacations so much that we forget to enjoy the rest of our lives, our day-to-day, moment-to-moment experiences. We plan and look forward to our vacations, sometimes as if they were the only part of life worth really living. We build up our expectations that our time off is going to be the highlight of our year, a saving grace that will make up for all the hassle and disappointment of our daily lives. We think to ourselves, "Boy, life is going to be great once we get there."

There are several problems with this overemphasis on vacation. First, as I have already suggested, vacation represents a tiny percentage of our overall lives. Most people I know spend a week or two, at most, on vacation. The rest of the time it's business as usual. To spend fifty weeks a year planning and longing for the other two is a classic example of reversed priorities, an exercise in almost guaranteed frustration. Part of the problem is that, when your primary emphasis is on later, your mind is removed from the present moment. Instead of being fully en-gaged in the here and now, and discovering joy in daily living, your focus is on how much better things will be and how much more fun you'll be having *later*—instead of now.

Another problem with extremely high expectations is that, in many instances, they are unrealistic, which can lead to a great deal of disappointment. Recently, Kris and I fell into this trap. It had been a particularly busy time and we hadn't had a chance to get away during the summer. We did, however, plan a mini-trip to the beach that we were really looking forward to. In my mind, this trip was going to be so great that it would make up for our lack of travel during the summer. I anticipated laughing children, appreciation for one another, and lots and lots of fun. However, what had been paradise in my mind turned out to be quite a hassle. It had been a while since all of us had been in one small hotel room together. It was crowded, and hot, and the kids argued more than usual. They disagreed about how we were going to spend our time, and Kris and I felt trapped in the middle. The beach was crowded and so was the pool, and the weather, of course, did not cooperate. In short, all of us realized that, at least this time, we really had more fun, space, and enjoyment back at our own home.

Please don't misunderstand me. I'm not suggesting that there's anything wrong with vacations or that looking forward to them is a mistake. I'm also aware that many vacations, including a vast majority of my own, are wonderful. What I'm attempting to alert you to is the common problem of making a bigger deal out of your vacations than is really necessary, of overemphasizing how great somewhere else is going to be instead of remembering how special and terrific your life is right where you are. I can guarantee you that if, instead of relying on your vacations to make you happy, you learn to be more contented and peaceful wherever you are, when you do get on your vacation, it too will be a rich experience—most of the time.

Of course, the reverse is also true. If you're unhappy and stressed out a vast majority of the time, it's unrealistic to believe that, once you get on vacation, you'll be relaxed and calm. My advice is simple: Go ahead and plan your vacation, and when you get there have a great time. But never forget that ordinary life can also become quite extraordinary if you remember to be grateful for what you already have.

62.

SPEAK WITH LOVING KINDNESS

It's easy to get into the habit of speaking behind the backs of others, speaking in a harsh or sarcastic tone directly to others, saying mean-spirited or negative things about life and other people, mumbling something disrespectful under your breath, gossiping, and other assorted varieties of negative speech. Unfortunately, this habit, as innocent and harmless as it may seem, does have some far-reaching consequences.

Setting aside, for a moment, the obvious fact that speaking harshly isn't a kind thing to do, let's consider some of the additional, perhaps less obvious, consequences. To begin with, speaking in a negative or harsh tone can be received as degrading or hurtful by another person. No one—especially our own family members—appreciates being attacked, and everyone almost always feels bad as a result. The act of being on the receiving end of a verbal attack encourages defensive reactions, even retaliation. There is no question that it detracts from the love in your home.

If the attack isn't direct but takes place behind the back of the other person, this too is a sign of disrespect. It doesn't give the person being attacked the chance to defend himself or herself.

But beyond all that, check in with how *you* actually feel when you speak in a harsh or negative tone. If you pay attention, I think you'll agree that it feels bad. Along with harsh words comes a feeling of stress and rigidity, a sort of unpleasant sickness in your heart. When you speak negatively, it focuses your attention on all that's wrong with the world and other people. It encourages you to forget all you have to be grateful for—and instead keeps you focused on imperfection. In short, no one wins, especially not you!

I learned this lesson very young. I must have only been a teenager when I said something (I can't remember exactly what it was) really mean to someone. But rather than responding with anger or becoming defensive, the woman said in a soft, gentle voice, "Do you feel better now that you've been mean and disrespectful?" I was stunned and felt like a complete jerk. Even in that painful and humbling moment, however, I learned a powerful life lesson that I have never forgotten— she was absolutely right. Rather than feeling cool or powerful, I felt like an idiot. I decided, right then and there, that I never wanted to be a person who said anything mean about another person. And while I'm sure I have deviated from that lofty ideal on many occasions, I do believe I have stayed relatively close to my goal. My recognition of how bad it felt to say something mean to another person has been a factor in keeping me from repeating this mistake too often.

Obviously, there are tremendous variations of harshness and differ-ent ways of expressing negativity with our speech. It can range from the truly hurtful to a seemingly harmless comment. I've discovered, however, that whether you're being cruel, on one end of the spectrum, or innocently negative or sarcastic, on the other, the effects are somewhat similar. If you catch yourself saying something mean (however slight), see if you go on to have a wonderful and peaceful day. My guess is that it won't happen very often.

There's a way in which speaking harshly (even slightly) disrupts the harmony of our day. It makes us feel a little off, negative, critical, and suspicious. But the reverse is also true. When the vast majority of our words stem from kindness and love, we feel an accompanying sense of peace and fulfillment, knowing we are doing our part in the creation of a kinder world.

No one is perfect, and we certainly all slip up from time to time. However, most of us (myself included) have plenty of room for improvement. I'll make you a deal. I'll do my best to speak with loving kindness as much as possible if you will too. If enough of us take this message to heart, we will all live in a more loving and patient world.

63.

SIT STILL

Do you ever take a few minutes to simply relax and do absolutely nothing, to just sit still? If not, you're missing out on one of the simplest methods of pure relaxation and a great way to prevent the accumulation of little things from bothering you too much. Often, we get so busy rushing around and so caught up in our busy lives that we forget how nice it is to simply sit still. If you've ever asked yourself what would constitute a simple pleasure, this is it!

Irrespective of how busy your life is or how many responsibilities you have, you probably have at least a few minutes each day to stop what you're doing and sit still. If you do, you'll experience some instant benefits that can make a world of difference in the quality of your experience. Sitting still provides a break in your hectic schedule, a chance to relax and recharge your mind and body. Sitting still gives you an opportunity to clear your mind and reflect, a chance for inspiration to arise. Often, one of the by-products of too much rushing around is that we feed into our reactive habits, therefore letting things bother us. What sitting still does for us is give us a chance to break any negative momentum that has built up during the day, an opportunity to regroup and start over. As you sit still and your mind quiets down, it's often the case that an answer to a problem will pop into your head, as though it came out of the blue. For some reason, the act of sitting still and quieting down has a calming effect on the nervous system that tends to bring forth wisdom and insight.

It would be very easy to dismiss this suggestion as being too simplistic. However, I've found that it really isn't. In fact, many of the best strategies to improve the quality of our lives are very simple. The problem is, we don't take the time to actually do these things. A few other "overly simplistic" suggestions might include: Get some exercise and plenty of sleep; eat lightly and healthily; think positively; avoid drugs and alcohol; and so forth. As simple as these well-known and very wise suggestions are, a very small percentage of us take advantage of their wisdom. Sitting still falls into this category—wise and simple, yet packed with potential value.

I'm not a doctor, so I don't know for sure, but my guess is that sitting still even for a few minutes may have some measurable health benefits. I know, for example, that when I sit still and do absolutely nothing, both my body and my mind feel calmer and more relaxed. My breathing seems to slow down and get deeper. My neck and shoulders relax a bit. Often, within a minute or two I feel refreshed and peaceful.

When you feel tense, and when you are rushing around, you are far more inclined to sweat the small stuff and get annoyed than when you are calm. Sitting still is not a magic pill, yet it is a reasonable facsimile. I've found that it's difficult to remain uptight once I take the time to sit down and be still.

This is undoubtedly one of the simplest suggestions I will ever offer you. It takes a few minutes, at most. It costs nothing and can be done anywhere. All you have to do is sit down and relax. I genuinely believe that if you give this strategy a try several times a day, you will be pleasantly surprised at how much easier it will be to take life in stride and go with the flow. What usually seems like a really big deal won't seem nearly as significant.

64.

TAKE IT AS IT COMES

One of the most important lessons I've *ever* learned is that life is rarely exactly as we would like it to be. Instead, life is exactly as it is. Nothing more and nothing less. And the closer we come to making peace with this fact of life, the happier and less stressed we will become.

One of the many ways to define unhappiness is the degree of difference between where you are and where you want to be—or the difference between what is and what you expect or demand. In other words, whenever something is happening, be it a fight between siblings, a broken television set, an embarrassing moment, or a leaky roof, you are faced with an important decision. Are you going to struggle and fight with what is actually occurring or are you going to accept it and deal with it?

Acceptance has absolutely nothing to do with apathy, not caring. When you accept what is, it doesn't mean you say "Oh, well, I don't care and I'm not going to do anything about it." It only suggests that, although you would prefer that things be different and you don't deny that you have a preference, you nonetheless recognize the futility of struggle. In a way, this form of acceptance of what is actually occurring in the moment is one of the ultimate forms of wisdom. It is one of the greatest stress relievers available to the human race.

One of the most difficult parts of parenting for Kris and me is when the girls are arguing or fighting. It's tempting to feel defeated, discouraged, and as though we're not doing a good enough job. It's easy to become bent out of shape or to yell out of frustration for the behavior to stop. However, in that moment, what is actually happening is that the girls are fighting. No amount of inner struggle on my part is going to make it any different. No mental anguish from Kris is going to make it go away.

Sometimes, Kris and I will look at each other in these moments and one of us will remind the other, "It is what it is." When this happens, it's inevitable that we will both lighten up and regain our perspective. Smiles will return to our faces. We'll remember that all siblings have quarrels and power struggles and that, while we may not like it, it's okay because it's part of the human predicament.

I'd like to reiterate that this peaceful acceptance is not about giving up or failing to make necessary changes. Life is full of adjustments, and all of us need to take action to improve our lives and strive toward our goals. If something is happening that you don't like and you can do something about it, great! Believe me, Kris and I do everything we possibly can to lessen the friction between the girls. But taking appropriate, heartfelt, and constructive action is an entirely different issue than becoming immobilized by the simple fact that life isn't accommodating us in exactly the way we would like.

Life is a journey. There are going to be ongoing issues to deal with and solve. So many things will occur that are beyond your control and that you disapprove of. This being the case, why not step back for a minute and see the wisdom of taking life in stride? If you do, your life is going to get a whole lot easier.

65.

STAY HEALTHY

I mentioned to a friend of mine that one of the strategies in this book was the suggestion to stay healthy. While she thought the advice was sound, she asked me, "But what does staying healthy have to do with not sweating the small stuff at home?" After I answered her question to her satisfaction, it occurred to me that many people might have the same inquiry because, on the surface, the two seem unrelated. They're not!

Think about what happens each time you, or someone in your family, gets sick. Whether it's a cold or the flu, one thing is certain to happen whenever you feel bad for an extended period of time: Your home begins to suffer, and so does your sanity.

To begin with, it's far more difficult to keep things clean and organized when you feel bad. It's also more difficult to attend to your responsibilities, as well as to the things you really do enjoy. Invariably, you fall behind on everything from returning phone calls, to spending time with your loved ones, to cleaning out your closets. And you'll probably agree that the more behind you get, the more tense you become. Your fuse shortens, and as it does, you get uptight and reactive.

The very same things that you ordinarily are able to take in stride begin to drive you crazy.

What this suggests, of course, is that your health is a factor in whether or not you're going to sweat the small stuff at home! I'm not suggesting that you become a health freak, or that you should use any lack of health as an excuse to sweat the small stuff. I am, however, suggesting that you might want to reflect on the overall importance of good health: things like proper hygiene, diet, nutrition, sleeping habits, adequate exercise, nutritional supplements, and other factors.

I once calculated that it would take several years of speeding in my car to make up for one full day spent in traffic school as a result of a speeding ticket. Looked at in this way, it makes little sense to speed. You can think of your health in a similar light. One additional cold or bout of flu that might have been avoided as the result of slightly better health habits will cost you far more time and effort than the simple steps you should take to become a little more health conscious.

Obviously, we can't control everything that happens to our bodies. However, for most of us, there is a great deal of room for improvement in the area of personal health. I urge you to consider this strategy as an important part of an overall improved life. I'm fairly certain that if you can become just a little healthier, you'll be less likely to sweat the small stuff—as much—at home.

66.

ATTEND TO FEELINGS FIRST

I first encountered this bit of wisdom in a beautiful book by Victoria Moran titled *Shelter for the Spirit*. She reminds us that things that seem important—dishes, cleaning, minor responsibilities, yard work, short-term goals, television programs, cooking projects, errands, and other day-to-day "stuff," while certainly relevant and unavoidable, can almost always, if necessary, be postponed. But, she points out, feelings cannot be postponed. They are right here, right now. And when they are present, you have only two choices— you can attend to them now or miss the opportunity and leave a potential scar. If you attend to them in a loving and respectful manner, you add to the love and rapport in your relationship—if you don't, you drift, however slightly, away from the person you love. While no single episode is likely to have a major devastating effect on your loved ones, there is certainly a cumulative effect that takes place, one way or another, depending on what you choose to prioritize most—feelings or things.

When I was a little boy, my father would respond to minor emergencies—things breaking, dents in the car, scratches on furniture, and the like—by saying "Relax. All *things* can be replaced—but *you* can't be." As an adult, I still remember how reassuring this message was to me as a child—and, to this day, I appreciate his loving words, because what he was really saying was that I (and my feelings) was more important than our "stuff." I try to keep in mind and implement the same philosophy when things are going haywire around my home. Although there's always plenty to do, I try, when possible (and when I remember), to put the emotional needs of my family (their feelings) first.

In a way, my dad's words and the idea of attending to feelings first go hand in hand. In both cases, we are reminded of the importance of keeping things in perspective—of not getting so involved or immersed in our things-to-do lists that we forget what's truly important. In other words, if your spouse, child, or friend wants or needs your undivided attention, it's generally a good idea to drop what you're doing (within reason) and offer your loving presence. Your child's desire to tell you a story, or your spouse's desire to share her day, are precious moments—opportunities to share and connect, to create memories. Your lawn may indeed need mowing, but it can wait. There are very few things I can guarantee. But this one I can: Your lawn's feelings won't be hurt if you wait an hour, or even an extra day, to mow it! Unfortunately, I can't offer that same guarantee when it comes to the feelings of your spouse or child.

I've found that it's extremely helpful to keep in mind that, ideally, feelings should be prioritized over practically everything else. When they are, you'll quickly discover that you'll have far fewer hurt feelings to contend with. And what's more, the lawn will get mowed just the same. This simple shift in perspective can make a world of difference in the love that is experienced and shared in your home. So before you rush out to mow that lawn, check in with your family and see whether a different type of priority may need some attention. You'll be glad you did.

67.

DON'T OVEREVALUATE
YOUR PERFORMANCE

Over and over I see people falling into this self-defeating trap that usually leads to frustration and dissatisfaction. Overevaluating your performance means you're keeping score of how you are doing. It means you spend time and energy thinking about how you're doing and how many mistakes you are making. You might say or think things like "Darn it, I've overacted to the kids four times today" or "It's been three weeks since the house has been really organized."

The problem with keeping score in this manner is that you'll rarely, if ever, feel as though you're doing well enough. By keeping track of your performance, you're focusing primarily on what you could be doing better. This puts added pressure on your already pressured life. It's like having a silent critic following you around the house all day long reminding you that you're not good enough. Even if, by your own standards, you're doing well, keeping score works to your disadvantage. It reminds you that you only deserve to be happy or feel satisfied when everything is in order.

A better solution to keeping track of how you're doing is to keep your attention fully in the present moment and simply make the decision to do the very best you can in every given situation. If the house is a mess and you want it cleaned up (and you have the time and energy), go ahead and get started. But notice how much more effective and less tired and resentful you become when, while you're working on the house, you avoid the tendency to remind yourself of how much of your time you spend cleaning or how useless cleaning is because everything will just be dirty again tomorrow. See if you can reduce or even eliminate the number of times you think about the *other* times you've spent cleaning. Instead, focus your attention exclusively on *this* cleaning effort.

My guess is that you'll be pleasantly rewarded by how much less effort it takes, and you'll feel much less overwhelmed when you take the evaluation factor out of the equation. You'll soon discover that any tendency you have to evaluate your performance is nothing more than a source of distraction that detracts from your productivity as well as from your overall enjoyment of the tasks of life. The identical process applies to dealing with your children, as well as dealing with other day-to-day activities. For example, rather than focusing on how many times you've had to break up an argument so far today, see if instead you can deal with this argument without the added burden of all the others. I'm sure this simple change in focus will make your life a lot easier to deal with.

There is something pleasant, even peaceful, about running a household, raising children, and dealing with life at home when your mind isn't filled up and overwhelmed with thoughts of how you are doing and how you could be doing better. By keeping the majority of your focus and attention on just this moment, you eliminate stress and increase your potential for productivity. You also increase the possibility of finding joy in the simplest of daily activities. So, stop wondering how you're doing and start really living!

68.

IMAGINE THAT SOMEONE ELSE IS IN
THE ROOM WATCHING YOU

Kris suggested this idea to me one day while I was clearly over-reacting to an extraordinary mess the kids were making. She said, ever so gently, "Richard, try to imagine that there is someone you don't know sitting down in this room observing your reaction." Despite the fact that, generally speaking, I'm the type of person who believes I have little to hide from others, her comment put things in perspective. Immediately, I recognized that I was making too big a deal out of the situation. I asked myself, "Would I really act this way if someone else was watching?" My answer: Probably not. The truth is, while I didn't like the mess, it certainly wasn't worth getting upset about. Better to spend my energy elsewhere.

This is an interesting and sometimes enlightening exercise to experiment with. The next time (or any time) you are feeling a little uptight or worked up about something at home, try to imagine that a stranger is taking notes on your behavior, perhaps in an attempt to learn an appropriate response. Doing so can be quite humbling and can act as one of the reset buttons discussed in an earlier chapter. It can quickly put things back into perspective by reminding you that you may be sweating the small stuff.

While I'm definitely not an advocate of basing our actions on what other people might think of us (to do so can be superficial and disingenuous), I do think there is some value in considering how we would *ideally* like to appear to others. This process can act as an internal barometer that serves to remind us of our own goals and values. For example, if you're frantically rushing around your apartment, cursing it for being too messy or not big enough, and you stop for a moment and practice this exercise, you might suddenly laugh at yourself and your obvious lack of perspective and gratitude. So if, like me, you sometimes get a little uptight around the house, do as Kris suggests and try to imagine how it might appear to others.

69.

KEEP IN MIND, AS WITHIN,

SO WITHOUT

This philosophical strategy has helped me many times throughout my adult life. It's greatest value is to help you regain your
perspective when your life seems hectic or out of control. It stems
from the understanding that your outer world—your environment, the
noise level, the relative calm or chaos in your life—is usually a reflection
of your inner world, the degree of peace and equanimity (or the lack
thereof) you experience in your mind.

Many people have a strong resistance to this strategy because it can
be quite humbling. Who wants to believe that a hectic life is caused,
even in part, by a frenzied mind? After all, it's easier to believe that
your life is hectic because of your circumstances, schedule, and responsibilities. If you have the humility to admit, however, that this message
is true, it can be enormously helpful, because while you have little control over your outer environment, you do have the capacity to change
from the inside out.

One of my favorite books is Jon Kabat-Zinn's *Wherever You Go,
There You Are*. Consider, for a moment, the essence of this title. It
correctly suggests that if you are nervous, hurried, and disorganized in

one home, you'll probably find a way to re-create a similar set of facts wherever you go. For example, have you ever met someone who is always late? Does it help if you give that person an extra ten minutes to get ready? No, it doesn't. The reason is simple: The habit that creates the tendency to be late isn't the clock, or the time of day, or even the number of things to do that day. Instead, it stems from an inner habit—the tendency to wait until the last possible minute to leave. You can change the external facts—where the person is going, who he or she is going to meet, and so forth, but the person will almost always find a way to show up late. He or she will always have an array of great excuses, but the fact remains; he or she will be late. This habit, like all the others, comes from inside the person and is reflected in his or her life.

The most helpful part of this information has to do with the question "What comes first, a calm mind or a calm life?" If you think about Kabat-Zinn's title, the answer, while difficult to admit, is obvious: A calm mind precedes a more peaceful outer life. In other words, if your life seems overwhelming, the best place to start your improvement is within your own mind. Perhaps you need a break or a change of pace. Maybe you need a little more time for yourself; maybe you need to spend less time watching television and a little more time reading helpful books. Would learning meditation or spending time in prayer be helpful? Perhaps you need less sleep or to get up even earlier to create some alone time. Each person is going to require a different prescription because each of us has different needs. Yet, the very act of simply acknowledging that the root of the problem lies within—not in the circumstances in your life—is often helpful in and of itself because it places the blame where it really belongs: inside each of us. The next time you're feeling overwhelmed or frustrated, slow down and take a look inside. If you do, I'm certain you'll agree that your outer life is a reflection of your inner world. By simply noticing this connection, you may very well know what steps are needed to solve the problem.

70.

CREATE A NEW RELATIONSHIP WITH
SOMEONE YOU ALREADY KNOW

It's quite common for us to get into habits with our family members and anyone else we happen to live with. These habits include, but are by no means limited to: overreacting, defensive communication, blaming, poor listening, expectations regarding behavior, and scattered attention. Indeed, it seems that the more we get to know someone—our spouses, children, parents, roommates, and others— the more likely we are to take them for granted, assume we know what they are thinking or how they are going to behave, react with a short fuse, as well as a variety of other knee-jerk responses. It's as if we expect the people we love and/or live with to behave in certain ways. We then validate those expectations by noticing the behaviors we are expecting to see and either ignoring or failing to see the rest.

As an example, for quite some time I found myself expecting my daughter to object to my suggestions regarding new activities that she might like to explore. I expected her to be somewhat resistant to my preferences, and it seemed that I was almost always right. I would suggest something—and she would say, "I don't want to." Due to previous experiences with her, and because of my certainty about the way she was going to respond, I discovered that I was actually looking for verification of my correct assumptions. I blew her responses way out of proportion and read into her motives, rather than seeing each situation with fresh eyes and an open heart.

I decided to try to create a new relationship with her surrounding this recurring pattern. I knew that the only way to do so was to explore *my* contribution to the problem instead of continuing to focus on her reactions. I looked at the ways that I was too aggressive with my suggestions and examined the ways I presented her with new opportunities. I discovered that the problem was, to a very large degree, me! Rather than motivating her, my genuine enthusiasm was overwhelming her. Her response to her feelings of being overwhelmed was usually to decide not to do something new. This invariably disappointed me, which encouraged me to get even more enthusiastic. You can probably imagine how much good that did. As I began to change, so too did our relationship.

The change in our relationship has been significant. I now understand that my expectations of my daughter, both for the way I felt she should respond to my suggestions and for my predictions regarding the way she was *going* to respond, represented virtually all of the problem. It turns out that she loves to try new things but prefers to do so in her own time—not mine. What she doesn't love is an overly enthusiastic father pushing her too quickly and demanding an enthusiastic response. Now that I can see what I had been doing, I don't blame her one bit! Because I have backed off from my expectations, she is now able to see that when I get too excited it's one of the ways that I show my love. Both of us are growing and becoming more accepting of the other.

In order to create a new relationship with someone you already know, it's critical that you attempt to let go of old hurts, sources of anger, and as many expectations as possible. It means total forgiveness and a complete willingness to start over. There may be someone in your life, perhaps many people, with whom it would be beneficial to create a new relationship. I encourage you to give this some genuine consideration. The rewards will be sweet and certain, and the nice part of it is, no one has to change except you.

71.

KEEP YOUR "THOUGHT ATTACKS"

IN CHECK

In every book I write, and every lecture I give, I try to include a little something on the subject of "thought attacks." Since home is such a potential source of stress for most people, this book will not be an exception.

We are thinking creatures. And because we're constantly thinking, it's easy to forget or at least lose sight of the fact that we are doing so. Instead, when we become lost in thought, our thinking is automatic. In other words, we are thinking about things—how much we have to do, how stressful our lives have become, how often we get stuck with the lion's share of the work, and so on—without conscious awareness that we are actively thinking.

The problem is, our thinking comes back to us in the form of feelings. What I mean by this is that if we're having angry thoughts, we feel angry. If we're having resentful thoughts, we feel resentful. If we're having hurried thoughts, we feel as though we don't have enough time. And if we're having stressful thoughts, we will feel stressed. Don't believe me? Just try to get angry right now without thinking about something that makes you angry! You can't do it. In fact, your feelings follow your thoughts just as surely as a lamb follows its mother.

Typically, a thought attack plays itself out something like this: You have a thought such as "This darn place is never cleaned up." In and of itself, this wouldn't be so harmful. However, we rarely have the wisdom to nip this thought in the bud. Instead, this single thought usually leads to other thoughts like "I'm the only one around here who does anything" and perhaps "I hate this place." Pretty soon, we're bothered and annoyed but don't realize the extent to which our own thinking has contributed to our mental anguish.

When this type of mental conversation takes place, only two things can happen. More often than not, the thinker (you) will continue to think this way until you begin to experience the stressful effects of those thoughts. Your train of thought may continue until you are distracted by a doorbell or a ringing phone.

Another option, however, is to catch yourself in the act of your thought attack—notice what's happening within your own thinking. Say to yourself, "Whoops, there I go again," or something else that reminds you that your thinking is about to drive you crazy and exacerbate any stress you are already feeling. When you become an observer of your own thinking in this manner, it allows you to nip your stress and frustration in the bud by getting you out of your head and back into the present moment. It helps you regain your perspective by not allowing your thoughts to make your life seem even more difficult than it really is. Obviously, the earlier you stop your thought attack, the easier it is to regroup and get back on track.

I can't tell you how useful this simple little technique has been in my own life and in the lives of thousands of others who have given it a try. You'll have fun with this one—but I must warn you. While the concept is simple, it's not always easy to implement. Once you start paying attention, you'll probably discover that you have a lot more thought attacks than you can possibly imagine. But the payoff is worth it. With a little practice, you'll be far more easygoing around the home.

72.

STOP EXAGGERATING

YOUR WORKLOAD

Despite the horrendous amount of work that must *actually* be done at home on a daily and/or regular basis, there is, nonetheless, an almost universal tendency to overexaggerate that which must be done and the amount of time we actually spend doing it. Before you jump on me and say, "That's easy for you to say; my workload isn't exaggerated," let me admit that I'm as bad as anyone else in this tendency. I've caught myself many times saying things like "I've been cleaning all day" or "It took me four hours to clean the attic." In reality, I may have been cleaning a few hours, at most, or piddling around in the attic for an hour to two. A friend of mine used to say things to her children like "I've been feeding you all day." And while it's true she had been involved with her children for most of the day, and while feeding them had been a significant part of the process, she now admits that the actual time spent preparing, feeding, and cleaning up the food amounted to around an hour and a half. This is significant because if you're overexaggerating the amount of energy spent on very many activities, it's going to seem pretty overwhelming, as though your entire life is filled up with nothing other than chores.

Unfortunately, it has become almost a sign of status to seem busier than everyone else, to complain to our friends, our spouses, and our children about all that we're doing. You virtually never hear someone admitting that he or she spent thirty minutes relaxing or reading a magazine on the couch, or that he or she spoke on the phone to a good friend for quite some time, despite the fact that these activities too, may also be a small part of your day.

At first glance, it might not seem to be that big of a deal to exaggerate a little about how much work there is around the house. But when you take a more careful look, you'll notice some surprising facts. When you exaggerate about how much you actually do, it puts a great deal of mental energy on the subject, blowing it a little out of proportion and making your life seem more difficult than it already is. It makes you feel sorry for yourself and creates a sense of helplessness. Exaggerating also contributes to both mental and physical fatigue by reminding you of how much there is to do, how much has always been done, and how little time there is to do it all. Finally, it takes away your sense of gratitude by encouraging you to lose your perspective and patience. In other words, rather than accepting taking care of your home as part of the overall package (that is, it comes with the territory), it encourages you to focus on the amount of work that is involved in having a home. You lose sight of the bigger picture and end up resenting what, in reality, is a privilege.

Again, let me emphasize that I'm not suggesting that there isn't a tremendous amount of work to do around the house. Believe me, I agree with you on this one! And I don't take anyone for granted, male or female, who does his or her fair share of this difficult, mostly taken for granted, work. However, the fact remains: If you avoid the tendency that so many of us have to overexaggerate that which we actually do, the amount of stress you experience pertaining to your home life will greatly diminish. You'll be able to appreciate the few breaks, and the time for yourself that you do get to enjoy, rather than focusing exclusively on the fact that your life is nothing more than one chore after another. Starting today, see if you can let go of that nagging tendency to exaggerate your workload so that you can focus a little more on the joys of living.

73.

REMIND OTHERS TO TREASURE LIFE

At the end of many of the letters I write, I use the salutation "Treasure Life" before signing my name. I also use these words, often, when signing a book for a reader and sometimes on my outgoing voice mail messages at work. It's one of the ways I try to remind people of the preciousness of life, of how lucky we are to be here, alive on this planet. When I use these words, I really mean what I say. In fact, I believed that gratitude is one of, if not the most important, tool for living a peaceful life. Gratitude has a way of putting almost anything into its proper perspective.

Too often, we take this incredible gift of life too much for granted. We rush around as if we have forever, respond out of habit instead of out of wisdom, and fail to attend to our highest stated priorities. We often fail to recognize and acknowledge not only what we have—a home, family, friends, possessions, and health—but life itself.

I have found that when I do acknowledge the gift of life, much of the "small stuff" that used to bother me takes on far less relevance and significance. Appreciation puts things in perspective and allows me to be less uptight and reactive. In fact, when I'm feeling really grateful, virtually nothing seems to get to me. Sometimes I can even see the humor in all the chaos.

When you remind others to treasure life, you can't help but do so yourself. Try it sometime. Remind your spouse or child, a friend, parent, neighbor, or someone else to treasure life, and observe what happens to you. You'll probably connect with the feeling of gratitude, of feeling blessed. The quality of your day—and of your life—will improve, as will the quality of life of those around you. Appreciation of life reminds you to be kind, humble, and generous and to take moments, frequently, to stop and smell the roses.

I encourage you to take this strategy to heart and implement it in your daily life. Remind others frequently to treasure life. Doing so will be a tremendous service to mankind and will help you as well.

74.

STOP REPEATING

THE SAME MISTAKES

Many years ago, Australian tennis star Ken Rosewall was asked his secret to success. In this particular interview he responded by saying, "I make a lot of mistakes, but I usually don't repeat them." The confidence he expressed in this answer has always stuck with me. I have found his message to be enormously helpful in my desire to reduce the stress I feel at home.

If you think about it, mistakes are really not that big of a deal. In fact, as most of us acknowledge, we need to make mistakes in order to learn and to grow. The problem, I believe, comes when we are unwilling to either acknowledge or examine the mistakes we make, thus leading to the tendency to repeat them—sometimes over and over.

One of my own ongoing mistakes was my insistence on answering the phone at home regardless of how busy I was. Sometimes I was doing two or three things at once, while already late to take one of the kids to school. Then the phone would ring. Rather than let the answering machine pick it up, I would compound my problem by answering it myself. Now there was someone on the line requiring my attention while everything else was still to be done. The person on the other end of the line would almost always sense my hurry, and would sometimes even ask, "Why did you even bother to pick up the phone?" I must have repeated this mistake hundreds of times before I finally got it. I have since stopped—and what a tremendous relief it has been! Because I was able to acknowledge the mistake I was making, I was able to make a simple adjustment in my habitual actions. Now, if I'm busy and the phone rings—it simply means the phone is ringing. I won't even consider answering it. This simple change has brought a great deal of peace to what used to be the craziest time of the day.

I've overcome many other repeated mistakes, such as getting too involved in my kids' arguments, trying to fit too many activities into a single day, waiting too long to clean my home office desk, and on and on.

Take a look at your own mistakes. The fact that you make them is no big deal! The more important question is, Are you engaged in *repeated* behavior and mistakes that you might be able to change? In most cases, the answer is yes. I can assure you that it's a very freeing feeling to admit to your mistakes and decide to make a change. That way, you won't be destined to repeat them.

75.

RECOGNIZE WHEN SOMEONE DOESN'T

HAVE AN EYE FOR SOMETHING

You may have heard the expression "He doesn't have the eye for it." In case you haven't, it means that the person you are referring to literally can't see what you are talking about; he or she can't understand or internalize it. For example, I remember trying to teach my oldest daughter to add two numbers together. Like the rest of us, before she saw how the principle of addition works in real life, she was stuck using her fingers and anything else necessary to add the numbers together. But, like magic, the moment it clicked, the instant she developed the eye for it, she was on her way.

Needless to say, it would have been foolish (and cruel) to get angry at her for not having the eye for math before she was developmentally ready. Instead, like most caring parents, my wife and I tried to be patient and allow her the necessary time to digest and understand the material.

It's easy to see how relevant having the eye for something is when we're talking about a five- or six-year-old's learning to add. It's something else entirely when we assume that someone should know something, yet it's every bit as important. For example, if you have a sloppy spouse, you probably assume (perhaps incorrectly) that he (or she) truly understands what it means to clean something up—or to live within a budget. You might make similar categorical assumptions about your children over such things as the meaning of quiet, patience, being nice, and other things you and I take for granted. The truth is, however, that many of the things we assume are general knowledge are nothing of the sort. In many instances, the problem *isn't* that a person doesn't want to, or is unwilling to, help but simply that he or she doesn't have the eye for what you are asking him or her to do. It's like you're speaking different languages.

When you take this possibility into consideration, your level of frustration will drop dramatically. Perspective and compassion will replace your demands and judgments. Rather than acting out from a place of stress, you'll be more likely to become a patient teacher, a participant in the process of helping another person develop the eye for something. The person you are dealing with will become much easier to work with. You'll be bringing out the best in him or her, rather than the worst.

My wife had an interesting realization about one of our favorite baby-sitters. Although she was an excellent sitter with the kids, we would come home from a night out and the kitchen would look like a bomb had just struck! We were constantly reminding her to clean up any messes she made, to which she would respond, "No problem." Yet, we'd come home to the same giant mess each and every time. We were getting very frustrated and were considering not using her again when Kris had the insight that the sitter might honestly *not know* what we mean by "clean it all up." To our great surprise, Kris was right. To our baby-sitter, the kitchen was as clean as it needed to be. Apparently, her own kitchen frequently looked messy. It wasn't treated as a big deal in her home. But to us, it was a big deal.

This story has a happy ending. Kris and I spent about thirty minutes showing her exactly what we expected and how to go about it. To this day, the kitchen has been spotless every time we've come home from a date. The secret wasn't to yell and scream or to get frustrated and fire her—it was to help her develop the eye for a clean kitchen. Experiment with this one and you'll solve many of your day-to-day issues, quickly and easily.

76.

DON'T EXPECT YOUR FAMILY
MEMBERS TO TREAT YOU
THE SAME WAY OTHERS DO

Over the years I've heard many people complain that their own family members treat them differently than everyone else. Most people seem surprised and disappointed that, at times, they are taken for granted, interrupted, not listened to, or treated with less respect than their family members' friends, colleagues at work, even complete strangers. Many people are also surprised that they receive more disapproval from family members than from anyone else.

If you want to have a more peaceful home life, it's critical that you get over this inevitable fact. Our own family members—the people we love the most—*do* treat us differently than other people. We see the best and the worst in our family members, and they, in turn, see the best and the worst in us. One of the reasons for this dynamic is that we feel most comfortable with those we are closest to. We are less guarded and feel we have less to lose. We feel safer experimenting with certain behaviors. In other words, we don't worry that, if we express anger, depression, or frustration, we are going to jeopardize the love we receive from our own family. It makes sense that we're not as frightened about losing it. After all, around our family we rarely, if ever, feel the need to put up a front or pretend to be what we are not.

Often, our family members can bring out the worst in us—they push our buttons like no one else. This innocent tendency is due to the simple fact of familiarity. Our family members are completely comfortable with us. Often, they see our potential as well as our weaknesses. Because they know us so well, they are more likely to see our flaws and our absolute humanness. Rather than struggle with this fact, we can learn to appreciate it. In a way, it's comforting to know that we can be ourselves—and be loved anyway!

Without a doubt, my children, more than anyone else, see the best and the worst in my behavior. Sometimes it's almost embarrassing to me—and funny to them—that I'm a person who teaches others to live a more relaxed life! Occasionally, I'll be leaving the house to teach a class or give a lecture shortly after an argument or disagreement with one or both of them. One time, my oldest daughter said to me in a sarcastic tone as I was leaving, "You just go teach them to relax, Dad." Ouch! But, of course, she was absolutely right.

The only way to move beyond getting upset about all of this is to *accept it* as par for the course—to know that it's the same for everyone else. Know that there are no exceptions and that it's okay. In fact, it's actually good for us. It certainly keeps us humble and, in some strange way, it's one of the things that makes family life so unique. Think about it. You'd probably never put up with strangers' speaking to you the way your children or spouses do! As you learn to accept, rather than fight, this family dynamic, you'll begin to see the humor and absolute innocence in it. You'll also begin to realize that you probably do the very same thing to your family members. So, relax and give your family members a break. Despite the way it sometimes feels, they really do love you, and their behavior is often a gift in disguise.

77.

GO CAMPING

On the surface, this may sound like an odd suggestion, but I'm absolutely serious! If ever you wanted a strategy that would virtually guarantee to help you regain appreciation for your home and its many conveniences, this is it. And, to top it off, you'll have fun too.

I have a friend who once spent a summer taking underprivileged children on backpacking and camping trips. The trips were designed to, among other things, heighten their appreciation for their everyday lives. He informed me that the trips were a smashing success. As the kids were exposed to the beauty (and hard work and inconvenience) of nature, they returned with a new sense of gratitude for the homes they had been blessed with—regardless of how simple their homes might have been. I've found that the identical result is achieved when I take my family on a camping trip that might be as short as a few nights. Invariably, we return home with a more humble and gracious attitude.

When you're out in the wilderness, the simplest things—the things we normally take for granted—are far more involved; cooking, heating water for coffee, getting comfortable and settled for sleep, cleaning up, taking a shower, and reading at night, to name just a few. In fact, something as simple as going to the bathroom can become quite a chore. Depending on where you are camping, you have to either hike to the bathroom or, in some cases, dig your own hole.

Don't get me wrong. Camping is loads of fun and, I believe, great for your spirit. Yet, it's loaded with work and inconvenience. Last summer, when Kris and I took the kids to a big redwood forest for our annual camping adventure, both children were eaten up by mosquitoes. They also missed their favorite television show as well as some of the books we couldn't fit in the car. Suddenly, our home didn't seem so bad after all—for them or for us.

One thing's for sure when you go camping. When you get home, you're really going to enjoy and appreciate a hot shower and a soft, comfortable bed. So, the next time you find yourself complaining about your home—for practically any reason—plan a camping trip and watch your complaints fade away.

78.

THINK IN TERMS OF MY CHILD,

MY TEACHER

Kris and I believe this concept is so helpful that we often repeat it to each other. The idea is to see your child not so much as an extension of yourself, or as someone you need or get to take care of, but instead as a human being who is here, among other reasons, to teach you about certain aspects of life that no one else possibly could. This strategy will help you learn from and appreciate your child more than you might have thought possible.

Regardless of their ages, our children *are* our best teachers. They have the capacity to teach us some of the most important lessons in all of life—things like patience, unconditional love, mutual respect, creative problem solving, accepting the inevitability of change, and taking life as it comes. On a day-to-day, moment-to-moment basis, our children are providing us with experience after experience, almost always with the potential to teach us something of lasting value.

Those of us with children know that nothing is more rewarding or challenging than the daily responsibilities of raising our kids. And many of us will admit that no one can push our buttons or test our emotions like our children. The next time your buttons are pushed, however, I'd like to suggest that you look at the situation a little differently. Rather than simply reacting as you normally do, try a little experiment. See if you can determine what lesson your child may be providing you. Ask yourself, "In what way is he/she acting as my teacher?"

I tried this strategy a short while ago and here's what happened. One of my buttons is when one of my kids talks back to me. For whatever reason, this has always gotten to me more than most of the other day-to-day challenges. My usual response to this disrespectful tone is to begin to lecture my child, which, as you might know, has minimal impact on current or future behavior. This time, however, I tried to look at it a little differently. I asked myself, "Is there something I can learn here?" and "Is there something she is unconsciously trying to teach me?"

I came up with a definite yes to both questions. I discovered two things. First, I needed to be far more patient. Because I tend to react so quickly to what I deem to be talking back, I tend to blow my daughters' comments out of proportion. In other words, when I'm more patient and take a step back, I notice that their comments aren't quite as disrespectful as I had imagined them to be—it's not such a big deal after all.

Second, I discovered that my daughter has learned to communicate primarily from her interactions with her mother and me. There are times that I'm not a very good listener, yet I seem to be insisting that she be one. As I looked at it honestly, I realized that she tends to be the most disrespectful when she doesn't feel listened to. What I've found is that I need to be a better role model, not a better lecturer. And I've already noticed that as I set a better example my daughter is less defensive and a sweeter child. Although each situation is unique, I think you'll discover tremendous value in seeing your child as your teacher.

Try this strategy the next time you feel frustrated with the behavior of your child and I think you'll agree: When you look at your children as potential teachers, the rewards for you, your child, and your relationship will be great.

79.

REMIND YOURSELF THAT
YOU CAN'T TAKE IT WITH YOU

Unless you know something I don't, when you die you will leave your home and *all* your possessions behind. Despite this rather obvious observation, many of us fail to live as if this were true. Instead, we spend a huge amount of our time and energy tending to—dusting, caring for, purchasing, insuring, protecting, taking care of, showing off—our stuff, as if it had some lasting value.

It's incredibly helpful to remind yourself that you can't take any of it with you! This doesn't suggest that you shouldn't enjoy your things while you're here—you most certainly should. Instead, it's s gentle reminder to keep things in perspective and ask yourself, "What's *really* most important here?" Ask questions like "Is it absolutely necessary that the bathroom get cleaned this very minute, or is it more important [and more nurturing] to take a walk with my spouse [or child or dog]?" Let me reiterate. I'm *not* implying that the bathroom doesn't need to be cleaned, only that it's helpful to keep its relative importance in mind. There will be times when cleaning the bathroom will take precedence over a walk in woods—and that's okay too.

I can almost guarantee you that someday, as you look back on your life, you'll be less interested in how many items and achievements you were able to collect than in how much you were able to express love, spend time with the people you care most about, and contribute to the world you live in. Acknowledging this truth *right now* can help you prioritize your goals and your time in a way that nurtures your spirit. It can be the difference between a superficial life and a life of substance.

Your home is an important part of your life. You live in your home. You spend a great deal of time there. You eat meals, share with family and friends, and rest—all at home. It's critical to remember, however, that the love we share in our home is what's most important—not the home itself, not the stuff. If something gets broken or needs repair, so be it. If the house is a mess or disorganized, do the best you can. Keep your reactions in perspective. Your things and your home are here to enjoy and to make your life easier and more comfortable. But don't give them the authority to overwhelm you. By reminding yourself that you can't take any of it with you, you open a new door of acceptance and freedom.

80.

HAVE A FAVORITE FAMILY CHARITY

Very few activities can bring a family closer together than the act of giving. We have found that having a favorite family charity is a fun way to do just this. Whether there are just two of you or ten, the idea is to get everyone in your family involved in the selection and ongoing giving process. (Obviously, if you live alone, you can do the same thing by yourself or with a friend.)

Our favorite family charity is Children, Inc., out of Richmond, Virginia; (800) 538-5381. It's an organization ideally suited for this purpose because it's easy to get everyone involved. Your family gets to meet, through the mail, a special child whom you all get to help and, and this is important, get to know. Both you and your kids can send letters, photos, and pictures back and forth to the child you are helping and meet a new friend in the process.

Almost any charity can be an ideal opportunity to bring a family closer together. Rather than simply writing a check and putting it in the mail, bring your family into the process. Get a corporate brochure and show your children who it is you're trying to help and why. Discuss the work that the organization is doing and applaud it together. If you are sending money, let the kids see you write the check. Maybe they can put the check in the envelope, or the envelope in the mailbox. Share with them where the money is going and what it is going to do. Ask your children who they would most like to help and why. Is it children, the elderly, the homeless, or the hungry? Or would they like to make a contribution to the search for the cure for cancer or blindness? Would they like to help stray animals or community development? This strategy gives your family the opportunity to discuss the needs in your community and in our world. It's a demonstration of your love. It's fun and rewarding, as well as helpful.

If you can't afford to give money, your family can still come together around giving. Perhaps your church or local shelter needs some help. A church in our neighborhood makes bag lunches for homeless people every Saturday. What a great way to spend a morning with your family.

What you do isn't as important as doing something. Giving of any kind feels good and brings people together, especially families. I hope you'll give this strategy a try. It will bring your family closer together and reinforce your most important values, and if each family does its own little part, we can make the world a better place.

81.

BE PATIENT WITH YOUR LANDLORD
OR BUILDING MANAGER

Whether you rent a room in someone else's home or have an apartment all to yourself, it's easy to become impatient and demanding of your landlord. The problem, however, with doing so is that your impatience may come back to haunt you. Not only do you have to live with the effects of impatience and of being annoyed, but also you'll lose the real-life advantage of having a landlord who is on your side.

Many years ago, while I was living in a large apartment complex, my roommate made the mistake of being consistently demanding and, I believe, obnoxious to the manager of our apartment building. He felt he was right and that his attitude was more than justified. He believed that our requests were not being adequately addressed, and in a threatening tone, he demanded greater service. Whether he was correct in his assessment or not was irrelevant to the end result. Regardless of who was to blame, he had made an enemy. The problem was, we lived in a college town where there were virtually no empty units. Essentially, we were stuck.

From that moment on, our slow service became almost nonexistent. If the furnace needing fixing, we were last on the list. When the refrigerator was leaking, it took weeks to get it repaired. If someone parked in our designated spot, it was our problem to solve—and the manager wouldn't get involved.

What my roommate didn't understand was that, in all likelihood, our manager had been doing the very best he could. We were living in a huge building that was rather old and in need of constant repair and updating. From his perspective, he was undoubtedly overworked and underpaid. And he was probably right. The factors he would have most likely used to create his priority list would have been, first, whether or not something was a legitimate emergency, and second, whether or not he liked the tenants who were making a request. Since our problems were always classified as nonemergencies, and since the manager no longer liked us, we were among the last on his list.

Obviously, there will be times when you may need to be aggressive or insistent that you get the service you deserve or require. However, whenever possible, try to reserve those instances to those rare occasions when it's truly necessary to be forceful. At all other times, try to be as patient and understanding as possible. As difficult as it can be to remember, landlords and managers have lives of their own, including many personal problems. I'm not defending landlords, nor am I at the time of this writing a landlord myself. I'm simply suggesting that it's *always* in your best interest to have your landlord on your side. If he or she is, more often than not, he or she will do anything within reason to make your life at home as comfortable as possible.

Dealing with landlords is one area where it's absolutely in your best interest to "not sweat the small stuff." The more perspective, kindness, and patience you exhibit, the more your landlord or manager is going to be inclined to be of service to you. The next time you have an issue to deal with that requires your landlord's involvement, try a little experiment. Let him or her know that you're aware of how busy he or she must be and how much you appreciate his or her help and hard work. Be kind, gentle, and patient. Do this not out of an attempt to be manipulative but simply because you are a kind, understanding person. Then sit back and observe what happens. You might be surprised at how much better your service becomes. Good luck.

82.

GET SOME EXERCISE

I'd estimate that at least half the people I know get little or no exercise. The excuses range from "I don't have time" to "It's too hard" and "I don't enjoy it."

While I'm certainly no expert on the advantages of exercise, I have enjoyed exercise for as long as I can remember. From my perspective, the only valid excuse for not exercising on a regular basis is the physical inability to do so. Other than that, as far as I'm concerned, if you don't get any exercise you're shooting yourself in the foot! You're missing out on an easy and effective way to become happier, less reactive, and more peaceful, and you're putting yourself at an unfair, yet totally unnecessary, disadvantage when having to deal with the inevitable hassles and challenges of life at home.

In a very real way, I feel I don't have time to *not* exercise—nor do I feel I can afford the luxury of not doing so. It would be very difficult for me to justify not doing something that makes me feel terrific and has the added benefit of keeping me healthy, fit, and calm—as well as providing me with tons of extra energy. Regular exercise has proven benefits of releasing endorphins, which have a calming effect on the brain and in your body. After exercising, many of the small things that drive you crazy would have little or no negative impact on you. And even the truly big things would be a little easier to deal with.

It's true that from a very narrow perspective, and in the very short term, exercise does take some time (I spend forty-five minutes to one hour, five or six days a week). However, that's an awfully small price to pay if you spend less time sick and/or in the hospital, and your day-to-day energy level and ability to be productive are increased substantially. It's also a small price to pay if you consider how much mental energy it takes to be annoyed and bothered by day-to-day things around the house. Just think how much better your life would seem if you could become even a little bit less reactive and more efficient as the result of getting a little regular exercise! Then there's your fitness to consider. To put it bluntly, a physically fit body looks and feels a lot better than one that is seldom used! Finally, while I can't prove this is the case, I know that I tend to sleep a whole lot better at night when I'm getting regular exercise.

I know, I know. It's hard to get started, and there are hundreds of great excuses. You should know, however, that in this past year alone I've met two incredible people—one in a wheelchair and another with very severe physical handicaps—both of whom are regular exercisers. Both also work full-time, and both have families to care for.

What have you really got to lose? I suggest and sincerely hope you'll give exercise a try—find something you enjoy: walking, jogging, hiking, biking, even running in place at home or on a treadmill. Do something. My guess is that, immediately, you'll be sweating the small stuff far less at home, and in time, you'll think it was one of the best decisions you've ever made.

83.

LOOK FOR

INCREMENTAL IMPROVEMENT

This is an attitudinal tip you can use in many aspects of your life, but it is particularly helpful around the home. It addresses the common frustration of feeling stuck, as if nothing ever seems to change.

The reality is, life is in a constant state of change. The problem is, we are usually too close to our own experience of life to see the changes that are taking place. An extremely common example of this phenomenon exists with children. If you are around them on a daily basis, you barely notice the changes. If a friend or relative who hasn't seen them in a while visits, however, they will usually say something like "My, how much the kids have changed."

Sometimes we get frustrated by problems that appear to be never-ending—bickering between the kids, a disorganized closet, a pile of unreturned phone calls, as well as so many other examples that can make life seem overwhelming. The mistake we make is that we're looking for perfection. Our expectation level is such that we fail to notice any incremental changes or improvements that may be occurring. We justify our own unhappiness because the kids *are* bickering, the closet *is* messy, and we *do* have phone calls to return. Our focus is on the problem and the obvious and never-ending lack of perfection.

The problem is, if we make the decision that we're only going to be happy when these (and other) problems completely disappear, we will have set ourselves up for a lifetime of disappointment. In reality, kids are always going to have some conflict, closets are rarely in perfect condition, and there will likely always be at least some phone calls to return.

It's extremely helpful to learn to focus not on perfection but on incremental improvement. Usually, if you look, you'll be able to find some. For example, the kids may indeed bicker, but perhaps not as much as last month—maybe it's a little better than before. Or maybe you were able to clean a tiny part of the closet, making it even a little less disorganized. Or you might notice that you were able to return a portion of your phone calls today, making the pile a little less overwhelming.

When you focus on incremental improvement, it will give you hope that there really is light at the end of the tunnel. It might even convince you that life isn't as bad as you can sometimes make it out to be. I think if you take a close and honest look at your life, you may be surprised at how often incremental improvements are being made. If you focus on these tiny improvements, it will reduce your stress and bring a great deal of joy to your life.

84.

REMIND YOURSELF FREQUENTLY
WHAT YOUR CHILDREN REALLY WANT

Let's face it. Your kids don't really care if you're a flight attendant, a salesperson, a waitress, a computer expert, or a chef. I can tell you from firsthand experience that they are not impressed if you are an author or a busy professional. My guess is that my kids would be equally *un*-impressed with me if I were a doctor, lawyer, or even a movie star. The fact that you work hard and sacrifice in their behalf may be appreciated, but not nearly to the extent that any of us feel is appropriate and deserved. No, what really matters to kids is your time—and your willingness to listen and love unconditionally. Period!

It's one thing to say "My kids are the most important part of my life," and it's something else altogether to back that statement up with actions. I know this isn't easy, and I also know that there are many great and often legitimate excuses why we can't make our kids our top priority, but the fact remains: Our kids don't want our external successes, they want and need our love.

This is not a strategy designed to make you feel guilty about how little time you have for your kids. Believe me, I often feel guilty myself when I have to leave for the airport before my own children have even gotten out of bed, or when I have to take an important phone call at dinnertime or miss a school play due to other plans. The goal of this strategy is not about guilt, it's about love. It's a friendly reminder that, although parenting can seem overwhelming at times and you might think it will last forever—it won't. Instead, you have a short window of opportunity in which to spend time together and develop a mutually loving and respectful relationship before your children are grown up and out on their own.

At times it's been helpful to me, and I believe it might be helpful to you, to be reminded that what our kids *really* want isn't our money or our success—or our constant reminders of how hard we work. What they really want is us. Obviously, this doesn't mean you don't need to earn a living or that success isn't (or shouldn't be) important, only that, to our kids, these things are secondary. I doubt very much that any of us, on our deathbeds, will wish we had spent even more time at the office or in pursuit of our dreams, but I suspect that many of us will regret not spending more quality time with our children. Knowing this is the case, why not make a change, however slight, in our priorities?

What our children really want (and need) is our love. They want us to listen to their stories without something else on our minds and without rushing to be somewhere else, to watch their soccer games not because we feel obligated to do so but because there is genuinely no place we'd rather be. They want us to hold them, read to them, be with them. They want to be the center of our universe.

Just this morning, I was with a good friend of mine discussing how quickly our children are growing up. It reminded me of how precious my own children, and all children, are. In that moment, I made a commitment to myself to keep my priorities straight, however inconvenient it may be. I hope you'll make a similar commitment.

85.

DON'T READ BETWEEN THE LINES

This is a common problem—especially at home. When we know someone really well there is an almost insidious tendency to think that we know what that person is thinking and/or how he or she is going to behave. This strategy is another way of saying "Don't be a mind reader, or a person who imputes motives into other people's behavior and actions."

I still find myself falling into this trap, although far less often than I used to. Just yesterday, for example, one of my daughters *appeared* to be procrastinating as usual instead of getting ready for school. Because I *expected* this to be the case, I noticed that her shoes weren't on and assumed she had no idea where they were. After all, this had been the case on many prior occasions. I, of course, knew without question what was going on! Impatiently, and with a sense of annoyance, I barked out, "Please go find your shoes." Her response was a confident "Daddy, my shoes are by the front door. You asked me not to wear them in the house." She was right on both counts. As is often the case for many of us, I had spent unnecessary moments of my morning being annoyed and bothered. My annoyance and inner stress stemmed not from anything my daughter was or was not doing but from my own thinking. This was clearly a case of "it's all in your head."

You can probably see that this tendency greatly contributes to sweating the small stuff at home. When you read between the lines, it's almost as though you're actively looking for things that bother and annoy you. And when you're looking for something, especially when you assume you're going to find it, you rarely disappoint yourself. In most cases, you end up validating your assumptions so that you can be right.

Obviously, an occasional assumption isn't going to ruin a relationship and is no big deal. However, this tendency is rarely occasional. Instead, it becomes a way of life—a habit, something we do a great deal of the time, often without even knowing we are doing so. Our mind works so quickly in its assumptions—what it thinks it knows—that it prejudges without any awareness on our part.

The solution is simple—but not easy. You must have the humility to admit that you don't know what someone is going to do or what he or she is thinking—you only think you do. It's important to take each day, each individual circumstance, as it comes. Don't assume that simply because something has always been a certain way there is no room for change. When you do, you display a subtle form of disrespect. After all, you probably don't appreciate it when someone you love reads your mind and predicts your behavior either.

When you make a shift from predicting behavior to responding to it, you'll find yourself being annoyed far less often. You mind will be more relaxed and present moment oriented—responsive to what is actually occurring instead of reacting to what you believe is going to be the case. In addition to the personal benefit you'll receive—less made-up stress—your loved ones will undoubtedly appreciate your shift as well. In many cases, this slight shift can make a world of difference in the feelings of mutual respect in a family.

86.

SPEAK SOFTLY

There is something nurturing and calming about someone who speaks very softly. For most of my life, I assumed that this was a quality you either had or didn't have—you were born with a soft voice or you weren't. And, to some degree, this may be true. However, in recent years I've discovered that speaking softly is a quality you can also develop. If you do, I think you'll agree that the rewards are tremendous and measurable. These rewards will have a positive effect on the love in your family and in your home.

When you speak too quickly and with a loud voice, the energy you send out into the world (or into your home) can be somewhat frantic or nervous. Although your intentions may be somewhat different, it's sometimes the case that the people around you will feel pressured or slightly agitated, which can, in turn, unconsciously encourage them to act even more hyper and irritated themselves. In other words, your voice feeds the cycle of nervous energy. It carries a great deal of power and authority and sends a message to those around you. So, if you send a message of impatience and agitation, you may be, without even realizing it, lessening the feelings of love, calmness, and respect in your home.

Obviously, everyone has a different voice, an individual temperament, and a unique communication style. I'm not suggesting that you (or anyone else) completely transform the way you speak, or that you pretend that you are someone you are not. What I'm proposing here is simply that you try to become a little more conscious about how your voice is being received by those around you. Further, I'm suggesting that if you make a gentle effort to speak a little more softly you might discover some surprising, almost instant, changes in the feelings around your home.

You, for example, will feel calmer and less stressed. As you quiet down your voice, you will actually relax the rest of your body, as well as your mind. Next, you'll discover that as *you* quiet down, everyone around you will quickly follow suit. This latter benefit happens almost like magic and is a welcome relief in any home. Although I have a long way to go, I've already noticed, hundreds of times, that if my kids are acting frenetic and silly and I want them to calm down, the very best strategy is for me to quiet down first. Often, calming down starts with my voice, which leads to calmer feelings and behavior. If you think about it, it makes sense that if you want others to behave in a relatively calm manner, the worst thing you could do is be yelling and acting crazy yourself. Yet, how many of us haven't done this? The truth is, if you really want someone to listen to you the best thing you could possibly do is to soften your voice. You'll be surprised at how attentive and respectful your audience will become.

By all means, honor your own rhythm and your own voice over my suggestions. However, if you give this strategy a fair chance, if you make an honest attempt to soften your voice, however slightly, I think you'll be pleasantly surprised at the calming effect it will have on your family and on your life at home.

87.

STAY PLAYFUL

As I reflect on the qualities of my family that keep us close to one another and on those memories that I hold dearest to my heart, up near the top of the list is that all of us are very playful together. Over the years, I've noticed a similar playfulness in many other families that seem truly grateful and happy to be together.

Being playful is a joyful quality. It keeps you laughing and smiling. It reminds you to not take yourself, or the other members of your family, too seriously. Being playful keeps you lighthearted and relaxed. It allows you to keep your heart open to those around you and to bounce back from setbacks. It removes much of the defensiveness that tends to occur in families and allows you to kid around with one another when appropriate. It also helps you stay connected when a heart-to-heart talk is in order.

It always seems so sad to me when I see people who have lost their sense of playfulness. They seem so serious, always on the verge of being upset and treating virtually everything as an emergency. Overly serious people often have a frown or look of disapproval on their faces and seldom experience the joy of simple things. Needless to say, people who aren't playful are constantly sweating the small stuff.

Being playful can mean anything from the ability to truly laugh at yourself to being open to new things. It can mean rolling around on the floor and roughhousing with your children or playing silly games with your spouse or tickling each other in the middle of the night. What you do isn't so important as the fact that you lighten up.

If you feel you've lost your sense of playfulness, don't worry—it's easy to get back. Start by smiling. Go ahead, give it a try. Then start to observe others who are playful. And rather than dismissing their behavior as light-minded, think of it as lighthearted. Being playful is innocent. It doesn't hurt anyone; in fact, it's a healing and refreshing attitude. As you observe others who are genuinely playful, notice how happy they are and how they bring out the best in others.

If you'd like to be more playful, you don't have to change your essential personality. Rather, take baby steps. Anything you can do to become a little less serious will be well received by virtually everyone you come in contact with. In fact, it can be the difference between someone's really enjoying your company and someone's keeping his or her distance. In addition, and perhaps most important, you'll find yourself becoming more philosophical and easygoing. The daily hassles we all must face won't seem like such a big deal and you will stop sweating the small stuff.

88.

THINK OF SOMETHING
YOU DID RIGHT TODAY

Just for a moment, think of how often you calculate, keep track of, or think about how many things you do wrong in any given day. Things like "I can't believe I misplaced my keys, showed up late for my son's class, forgot to pick up sandwich stuff, missed the first ten minutes of the soccer game, forgot to make that important phone call, messed up, dropped the ball, failed to deliver, made her angry," and on and on.

Now, shift gears and think about how often you give yourself credit for doing something right. If you're like the vast majority of people I know, your ratio of criticisms to compliments is going to be weighed heavily toward the negative.

You might be thinking, "Oh, everyone is like that. What's the big deal? It's only human." This assumption is partially true. Unfortunately, most people *are* like that. Most people do focus excessively on their mistakes and pitfalls. But that doesn't make it a good idea. The problem is, most people don't understand the price they are paying for this excessive focus on the negative. The price I'm referring to is stress and an uptight, self-defeating, and rigid experience of life.

Life is full of mistakes. There are simply too many things to do, and attend to, to avoid mistakes and do everything perfectly. In order to maintain a sense of equilibrium, you must give yourself a break and make allowances for the reality of imperfection. In fact, if you did everything perfectly, life would truly be boring.

Focusing on what you do wrong encourages you to sweat the small stuff. It puts your attention on all that is wrong with yourself and the world and makes you feel less than okay, even incompetent. Negative focus generates negative energy and, I believe, feeds into negative behavior. It reminds you of problems, hassles, and inconveniences. It makes you feel uptight and encourages you to be critical and hypersensitive.

When you think of things you do right, however, it brings your focus back toward the good in yourself. It reminds you of your competence and good intentions. It encourages you to give yourself a break and to make allowances for the few little things you do wrong or need improvement on. When you remind yourself of the things you do right, it helps you become a more patient person, with yourself and with others. It helps you recognize the effort and overall positive batting average that most of us experience, the fact that, despite our mistakes, we do most things pretty well. Rather than seeing yourself as a mistake maker, you'll see yourself (and everyone else too) as a character who is doing the best you know how.

Perhaps more than all of this, however, is the fact that focusing on what you do right makes life a lot more fun. It makes you less serious and rigid, and helps you feel less pressured, as if someone is keeping score of your efforts. My suggestion is this: Do the best you can in all aspects of your life, and then let go of it. Regardless of how hard you try, you're still going to make your share of mistakes. Once you accept this fact of life and put more attention on your strengths than on your weaknesses, you'll start having more fun than you ever dreamed possible.

89.

DISCOVER A SIMPLE PLEASURE

I've found that the best things in life, while not always free, are often very simple (and almost free). Without question, discovering a simple pleasure is a wonderful way to add more joy and peace to your life.

My wife, Kris, has a simple pleasure that serves as an excellent example. Each year, she plants several rows of sunflowers, the kind that grow really tall, in our backyard. I have never seen anyone love flowers more than she loves those sunflowers. Several times a day, she takes time out to look at and appreciate them. She takes great pleasure in watering and caring for her prized flowers. And when the time is right, she cuts them, a few at a time, and brings them into the house for everyone to enjoy. She often gives a bouquet to friends or family when they come for a visit, and this too brings her great satisfaction.

As you can see, this simple pleasure does far more than provide beauty to our yard and family room. It brings tremendous joy to Kris's life, and that joy extends well beyond the moments she is actually with them. In a way, her flowers act as a source of grounding to her entire day. She looks forward to seeing and caring for them. She smiles when she thinks of them, and I think they help her keep her many responsibilities in perspective. And although she doesn't maintain this simple pleasure for any ulterior motive, it *is* really nice to see the effect this tradition has on our children. They get to see their mother genuinely enjoy something simple and beautiful. They witness her appreciation firsthand and, I believe, are more inclined to be appreciative themselves as a result.

If you take the time to think about it, you'll almost certainly be able to think of something that can act as *your* simple pleasure. For me, it's taking time to browse in a bookstore or to drink coffee by myself in a coffee shop. I also love to read, wrestle with my kids, and jog in the park near our home. These are a few of the things that bring me the greatest joy. And I believe that the more joy we have in our lives the more able we are to keep our perspective, maintain a relative state of calm, and *avoid* sweating the small stuff.

I hope you'll take the time to think of at least one simple pleasure you can enjoy. Whether it's a few minutes of quiet reading, taking a course for no other reason than a desire to learn something new, or taking a walk or a drive, it will pay tremendous dividends.

90.

REMEMBER, IT'S THE LITTLE THINGS
THAT WILL BE REMEMBERED MOST

Recently, I was in the midst of an extended promotional book tour and had been on some very exciting national television and radio shows. I had been speaking to huge, enthusiastic audiences and was being treated extremely well by my publisher, the public, and everyone else. At the time, I had the #1 best-selling book in America, *Don't Sweat the Small Stuff*, and had been sincerely honored by the reception of my work. Everything was wonderful except one thing—I deeply missed my daily routine of spending time with my family.

One night I called home and my two girls sang to me over the phone, simultaneously telling me how much they loved me and couldn't wait until I got home. They were carving pumpkins for Halloween and promised to save the biggest one for me. As I hung up the phone in the Chicago airport, I began to cry. My tears were a mixture of joy and sadness, of being so deeply touched in the heart that I couldn't contain my emotions. I realized that no matter how wonderful your life is, what your hopes and dreams might be, or what's happening in your career and other aspects of your life, it's the little things that matter most.

That night, as I flew to Hartford, Connecticut, for another show, I reflected on my fondest memories. And guess what? They weren't our most exciting vacations or my greatest achievements. Although these external things are important to me, the memories that really stand out are those that touched my heart—like the time I was really upset about something and my youngest daughter, Kenna, sensed my emotion and gave me a big bear hug and told me, "Daddy, everything is going to be all right." She was four years old. Nearly two years later, it's as if I can still feel that hug and hear her words of encouragement. Then there was the time my daughter Jazzy and I had the worst kind of flu at the same time. We spent the night together, comforting one another, suffering through it together. (I'll spare you the details.) But, at some point, she gave me one of the sweetest looks I've ever seen, and in a soft little weak voice she said, "Daddy, I'll never forget this. Thank you for being with me." She will never forget that experience, and neither will I. It was absolutely worth having to go through the worst flu of my life to hear those words.

To me, this is one of the most important points in this book. It's tempting to spend your life hoping it's going to be better later. Most of us look forward to promotions, special events, vacations, and high-lights. And certainly these are wonderful things to anticipate. Yet, if we focus too much on these somewhat rare instances, we can miss out on the ordinary, yet incredibly special, events that happen on a regular basis—the beautiful smiles and laughter of children, the witnessing of simple acts of kindness, sharing a beautiful sunrise or sunset with some-one you love, or witnessing the changing colors of the trees in the fall. These are the things life and memories are made of.

If you remind yourself to look for and appreciate the little things, your power of observation will be heightened. You'll begin to see "ordinary" experiences in a far more extraordinary manner. If you take a few moments to reflect on what truly matters in your life, I think you'll agree—in the end, it's the little things that matter most.

91.

BE AN EXAMPLE OF PEACE

The old saying "Do as I say, not as I do" doesn't work very well at home! What does work, however, is the reverse, or "Do as I do, not as I say." Whether you live alone, with one other person, or with many, the most effective way to create a more peaceful home environment is for you to become an example of peace.

The emotional climate you live in begins with you—as mine does for me. If you are agitated, nervous, frantic, and frustrated, it's unrealistic to expect that the other people in your home are going to thrive. Instead, they will likely be walking on eggshells trying not to upset you. Any negativity you harbor will affect, to some degree, the others in your home (not to mention the effects on yourself). This doesn't mean that it's your fault if your home is less than peaceful, only that in most instances, if you wait for others to set the example you'd like to see, you're going to have a very long wait!

However, when you are calm, patient, and loving, you bring out the best in those around you. By being an example of peace, you open the door for others to be more patient, accepting, and gracious. Rather than being upset by the ups and downs of daily living, you create an environment in which it's okay to go with the flow. And the calmer you become, the easier it is to make the necessary adjustments to the complications and challenges of daily living. By being peaceful, you eliminate many of the mental distractions that interfere with your wisdom and common sense, thus making it easier to see solutions instead of problems.

The first step in becoming calmer yourself is to acknowledge this goal as a priority in your life. Instead of waiting for others to step forward and blaming them for the chaos in your home, make the decision to have peace as *your* top priority—decide it's a goal worth striving toward. Practice the strategies in this book as well as others that resonate in your heart. I think you'll discover that when peace is your primary goal most everything else will fall into place and will be much easier to deal with. In addition, you'll be setting the stage for others to live a more peaceful life, which, in turn, further reduces the chaos you must live with. Becoming more peaceful might not happen overnight, but it is certainly a goal worth striving for. Beginning now, you can make choices that lead you in this direction.

92.

EXPRESS GRATITUDE FOR YOUR HOME

This is one of the easiest suggestions to implement in this entire book. Yet, it is so powerful that it's worth doing—starting right now. Think about your home for a minute. Whether you live in a tiny apartment, a room in someone else's house, or your own home, it's yours to use. It's your space. What in the world would you do without it? How would you survive?

It's remarkable to reflect on how fortunate you are to have a home, a place to rest, a haven of potential peace. But when was the last time you slowed down enough to really look around? Notice the walls, the overall environment, the floors and windows. When was the last time you consciously expressed gratitude for your home? I've met many people who have never, ever, taken this step of thanks.

Take a deep breath and express gratitude for your lovely home. Despite its imperfections, it's yours. You live in your home. It protects you from the elements of hot and cold, and against everything from insects to strangers. It helps keep you alive and comfortable. Yet, for the most part, it is taken entirely for granted. Sure, sometimes we'll say "Thank you" as a routine part of a prayer or ceremony. But what I'm suggesting here is quite different. I'm asking you to take a few moments every day, for the rest of your life, to quietly reflect on the joy of having a home—whatever it looks like and however hard you work to maintain it.

Taking part in the expression of gratitude does many things. It puts your attention on how lucky you are instead of all that needs to be done. It helps to keep things in perspective. When times are difficult, it reminds you that, despite the difficulty, you are indeed fortunate to be alive and to have a home. When you are overwhelmed by the work involved in having a home, or by the cost or all that goes along with it, gratitude will help keep you pointed in the right direction. Gratitude is a very powerful emotion. It brings forth the best in you and helps you maintain your emotional bearings. It helps you be happy.

If you're at all like me, you're going to be amazed at how good you'll feel the first time you take part in this exercise. You'll probably wonder why you haven't been doing it all along. Enjoy the feelings of gratitude and, perhaps for the first time, really enjoy the privilege of having a home.

93.

STOP COMPLAINING ABOUT

THE COMPLAINING

Being a parent, I've learned a lot of interesting things about children. But one thing stands out: Children and complaining go hand in hand! From the day your child is born, when he or she cries and complains out of pure need, to the day your teenager moves out of the house and complains that his or her stereo isn't good enough, you may never again experience a day without at least some complaining to deal with.

Someone once told me that the reason our children and other family members complain so much is that they feel most comfortable with us. Upon reflecting on this comment, I realized that sometimes I wish my family *wasn't* so comfortable with me! I'll bet there are times when you feel the same way.

I've observed two consistent dynamics about complaining that I feel may be useful to share with you. First, listening to other people complain feels stressful and encourages me to complain myself. For example, suppose it's hot outside and I'm already uncomfortable. Now, one of my daughters begins to complain about how hot and thirsty she is. This reminds me of how uncomfortable *I* feel and I immediately begin to wish she would stop bringing it up. But kids will be kids. She says it again, and again, and again. Pretty soon, I'm so tired of the complaining that I complain to my wife, "The kids are always complaining." So, my first observation is that complaining brings on more complaining.

The other observation I've had about complaining is that never once has my objection to the complaining stopped it! In fact, it seems that it makes matters worse. It gives the complaining additional energy and feeds the cycle that already exists.

In recent months I've made great strides in this area, and it's been easier than I dreamed possible. Rather than complaining about the complaining, I've decided to make peace with the fact that listening to complaining is a fact of life. And to be completely honest, I've discovered something truly remarkable: The complaining has lessened substantially. It's not getting to me nearly as much and there seems to be far less of it to contend with. The fact that I've become less emotionally invested in the complaining has made complaining less appealing to my kids. So, my advice is simple: As difficult as it may be at first, and as justified as your own complaints may seem, try to stop your part of the process. My guess is this: If you stop complaining, those complaints that you are forced to listen to will gradually disappear. Good luck on this one, but don't complain if it doesn't help!

94.

EMBRACE CHANGE

Embracing change is always important, but never more so than at home. The truth is, everything is in a constant state of change—our bodies, the physical structures of our homes, and our children are aging and going through an ongoing state of change. The way we look at age twenty is quite different from the way we look at age forty, sixty, and eighty. Likewise, as our children grow older they are constantly going through major changes—physically and emotionally. Needless to say, your cuddly four-year-old son is going to be a very different person when he is a young teenager, and different still when he turns eighteen.

We have two choices when dealing with change. We can fight and resist—or we can surrender and embrace. Most people resist change with all their might. They fight against aging, shifts in family tradition, changing attitudes in their children, and virtually all major changes in their lives. The problem with resisting change is that it's a losing battle—100 percent of the time. Change is one of the only certainties in life, one of the very few things you can count on. When we resist the inevitable, we cause ourselves a great deal of pain and sorrow and we miss out on a great deal of potential joy. For example, I've met many people who spent so much time and energy fearing their fortieth or fiftieth birthday that it was almost as if they missed the few years that preceded it—their attention was somewhere else. Other people are so unhappy that their children are growing up and leaving the nest that they fail to appreciate the last year or two that their son or daughter is still at home. Still others get depressed or bothered over slight shifts in family traditions—someone changes the Thanksgiving menu, or suggests Christmas in a new location, or something else that alters the status quo.

I'm not suggesting that you surrender blindly to the aging process and fail to take adequate care of yourself—or that you don't work to preserve traditions that you truly enjoy. What I'm referring to here is becoming upset and frustrated over changes that you have no capacity to control. Go ahead and enjoy one phase of life—but not at the expense of all the others. Instead, enjoy the next phase just as much as the last. Open your heart to what is in front of you and you may find that adjusting is easier than you think.

When you embrace change, you open the door to a far more peaceful existence. Rather than insisting that life be a certain way, and that it stay that way forever, you begin a journey that includes acceptance and appreciation for each phase. Then life becomes more of an adventure and each step seems special and important.

95.

REVERSE ROLES WITH YOUR SPOUSE

It's sad, yet the easiest person to take for granted is probably the person you love most in the world—your spouse. It's so easy to get lost in your own world and set of real-life responsibilities that you begin to believe that your spouse has it much easier than you do, or you forget (or perhaps don't even realize) how hard your spouse works in your behalf. This tendency can create a great deal of resentment yet is, to a large degree, very preventable. The key to prevention is to put yourself in your spouse's shoes.

I'm going to give an example here *knowing* that there are millions of exceptions to this stereotype. I'm aware that in today's world many, if not most, families have two income earners and that many, if not most, families share many of the responsibilities at home. I'm also aware that women are often the ones who work while men stay home with the kids. See if you can see through my stereotypical examples, however, to the heart of this important message.

Many of my own male friends have fallen into the trap of taking their spouses for granted. I'm happy to report, however, that some have been helped by taking this strategy to heart. A common example is a man who works and is married to a woman who stays at home (and of course she works hard too). In this typical chauvinistic example, the husband convinces himself that his wife is lucky and often minimizes the importance of her role. He believes her needs are being met while he's out working all day. He rarely contributes much at home in the way of chores, children, and household responsibilities. He feels put out when asked to do the simplest of things. He's absolutely aware of how hard he works but takes his wife's role completely for granted.

It's shocking (but often very good for a marriage) in cases like this for the husband to take over the home for a week, or even a few days, while his wife visits friends and takes a break. Many men are so frightened by this suggestion that they get the point before they are actually forced to go through the experience. They often realize, when push comes to shove, that they are absolutely incapable of doing the important daily tasks of running a home and raising children. They also realize how exhausting it can be. This is truly hard work! The idea, of course, in switching roles is to regain a sense of gratitude as well as compassion for what one person does for the other.

Of course, this strategy works both ways. It's also very common for a stay-at-home mom to take her husband for granted. She might, for example, complain about late nights or missed dinners without fully realizing how difficult it can be to earn a living. In most instances, it's unrealistic for a nonworking spouse to actually reverse roles for a week. However, she (or he) could really benefit from trying to imagine what it would be like to actually go out and earn enough money to satisfy the financial needs of her (or his) family. This can be a shocking realization for someone who doesn't actually have a job.

The point of this mental exercise is not to determine whose job is more difficult or important but to recognize the importance and inherent difficulty in both aspects of life. Regardless of your personal situation, and even if you and your spouse both work and both help out at home, it can be enormously helpful to experiment and play around with this strategy. If you do, I think you'll begin to realize and appreciate how much your spouse does for you and how difficult his or her life can be at times. And I can assure you that everyone loves to be appreciated; when people are appreciated, they are more fun to be around.

96.

SURRENDER TO THE FACT THAT
THERE'S ALWAYS SOMETHING TO DO

Sometimes making peace with the obvious is enormously help-ful in preventing you from becoming overwhelmed or resentful. There are many observations about life that fall into this category, including: There's never enough time to get everything done; some-one always has something you don't; you can't be in two places at the same time; there are trade-offs in life; tax day is April 15: you are going to get older and eventually die; you can't be all things to all people; and, of course, there's always something that needs to be done around the home!

For some reason, perhaps because these obvious things are so close to us, many of us tend to struggle against them. It's very common to hear people saying things like "My house is never the way I like it" or "No matter how hard I work, I can't get everything done." I have found it to be incredibly useful to surrender to certain aspects of life that are absolutely predictable. Near the top of this list is the fact that, regardless of where you live, who you are, or how much money you have or don't have, there's *always* something to do. No amount of complaining, simplifying, wishing it were different, or clever planning is going to change this simple fact of life. I have discovered that the best way to deal with this issue is to surrender to the fact that it's always going to be this way. I've known a number of people with virtually no money, a handful of people with all the money they could possibly need, and a huge number of people who fall somewhere in between. And no one, not a single person, has ever been exempt from this rule of life.

A few weeks ago, Kris and I spent a Saturday around the house trying to catch up on a few of our unfinished projects. As I looked around, I was shocked at how much we had to do. There was laundry to be done, floors to be washed, closets to be cleaned, and an attic that needed to be organized. My upstairs office looked as if I hadn't opened my mail in months, despite having sorted through it just the day before. The hamster cages needed to be cleaned, and the front porch was in need of sweeping. Of course, the kids' rooms required their daily attention, and our own bed needed to be made. The dog needed to be taken on a walk, and my younger daughter's bike seat needed to be raised. On top of all of this, the plants, both indoor and outdoor, needed watering.

Obviously, this was the mere tip of the iceberg. This simple list doesn't include the basic day-to-day stuff of life like paying the bills or reading to and spending time with the kids. Nor does it take into consideration the fact that the kids eat three meals a day, which take preparation and cleanup time. It also doesn't include major maintenance items, such as the fact that our home needs painting, or that there are many things such as appliances and garden furniture that are worn out and need to be fixed or replaced. It also doesn't account for the lawn that needs to be mowed each week and the rest of the garden that has accumulating weeds. I could go on, but I know you've got the picture!

When you step back for a moment, you can probably see how easy it can be to become discouraged (if not driven crazy) by all there is to do. If you decide you won't rest until everything is done, you will spend your entire lifetime very tired and frustrated. It's easy to sweat the small stuff at home because there is so much small stuff to contend with! The only way around this problem is to surrender, let go. Make the decision that it's okay to do your best even though it's a battle that, ultimately, can't be won. The best you can hope to do is stay on top of things, prioritize what's truly important, and maintain a sense of humor. In short, you can only do what you can do. Coming to the realization that inherent in life is the fact that you'll never be able to get everything done is not a defeatist attitude. It's simply an acknowledgment of the truth. The very fact that you're doing one thing suggests you aren't doing something else. So, starting today, give yourself a break. Relax. Do what you can but don't beat yourself up. You'll be much happier as a result.

97.

BECOME CLUTTER-FREE

As simple as this suggestion is, it's worth discussing. And as simple as it sounds, it's actually not an easy task. It's taken a great deal of persistence, but I'd estimate that I have eliminated more than 90 percent of the clutter in my life. I'm convinced that this effort has helped me immeasurably in becoming a more easygoing person, as well as in my desire to stop sweating the small stuff at home!

Virtually every day, different forms of "stuff," much of which is useless and only takes up physical and mental space, comes into our lives. Without a concerted and conscious effort to counter this accumulation, we end up with piles and piles of useless junk to contend with. The reason: Clutter comes into our life whether we want it to or not. So, if we don't have a method of getting rid of at least as much (on average) as is coming in, it's inevitable that the piles will become ever larger and more difficult to sort through. Many people fool themselves that they will "get to it soon" or fall prey to the (almost always) false belief that they may need it someday. This latter excuse is validated by remembering a time or two when they needed something and found it buried under stacks of boxes in the back of the garage.

Clutter includes anything and everything that takes up space, distracts our attention, is irritating and in the way, or is practically never used. Some of the most common forms of clutter are piles of junk mail, scraps of paper, old newspapers, phone books, magazines, clothes and towels we no longer use, gifts and other items we don't know what to do with, old bikes and exercise equipment, piles of unused scrap lumber, nondeductible receipts, keys we no longer need, toys the kids never ever play with, old letters and other mail, books that we have either read or don't intend to read, memorabilia and other so-called sentimental things, knickknacks we don't even like to look at, excessive dishes or pots and pans, silverware and other kitchen goods, and so forth. When you get right down to it, most homes are filled to the brim with stuff that does little else than fill up space. I've been in many homes where the closets were absolutely filled up with things that were never used and where there wasn't even an intention of using a single item in the closets. And when I've been brave enough to ask the question "Why do you keep all this stuff?" the answer was usually something like "Oh, I don't know, we've always had it."

I believe that the reason so many people end up letting clutter take over their lives is that they have never felt or experienced the joy of a clutter-free home. Most people, in fact, had parents who did precisely the same thing. Often, the first time an attic is cleaned out is when a person dies or is forced out of a home for health reasons.

There is, however, something incredibly peaceful about a clutter-free home: opening a closet and actually having space to hang up something; opening a drawer without having to use force; being able to find virtually everything you look for; having open, airy space where there is nothing at all. There is something effortless and pleasant about sitting at your desk and being able to see the surface and to find your address book. There is something equally freeing about opening a kitchen cabinet and being able to choose easily and quickly from your favorite pots and baking trays without having to sort through and push back as if you were trampling through a thick forest.

Becoming clutter-free is an easy way to simplify your life and to feel more organized and in control. It gives you a peaceful feeling of space. It lifts your emotional spirit by giving you a feeling of openness and of being connected to, rather than overwhelmed by, life.

You can begin in simple ways—empty out drawers and closets. Give things away to people who will actually use them. Have a garage sale, and rather than keep the things you don't get rid of, give everything that's left to your favorite charity. Cancel any magazines you don't actually read and recycle all the ones you have kept. Go through your sentimental things and create *one* special box for the things you'd really like to save—and give everything else away. Go through your clothes. Do you really wear them all? If no, wouldn't it be nice to give the things you don't wear to someone who will? And couldn't you use the tax deduction anyway? Maybe you could implement a new clothing rule: If you haven't worn it in two years, give it away today!

Most people who try to simplify their lives in this way are thrilled at the result. For some, it becomes a way of life that seems easier to manage. For others, it's simply an exercise in making their lives a little easier. I've found that as I accumulate less and get rid of the things I don't actually use, I truly appreciate those things that I do decide to keep. I hope you'll give this strategy a try, because if you do, my guess is that you'll be glad you did.

98.

DEFER GRATIFICATION

At first glance, this suggestion may appear more suited for work or money-related issues than it does for life at home. However, if you look closely, you'll see that the identical principle applies in both cases. I've been rewarded again and again by taking this strategy to heart around my home.

To defer gratification means you either do something you may not necessarily want to do or give something up now so that you will be rewarded later. You defer or postpone your gratification because, presumably, the deferred reward is greater than the present cost or effort.

One obvious application of this strategy lies in dealing with your kids. You might, for example, desperately want your cranky child to take a nap. However, if it's five P.M., you might be wiser to stick it out and put him or her to bed for the evening at seven. If you allow the child to take a nap now, he or she will likely be lively and rested when you are ready to go to sleep for the evening, perhaps keeping you from getting the sleep you need. In this case, you are postponing your gratification (your quiet time) for a few hours so that you won't have to endure a sleepless night. Or your child might be crying because he or she wants a big bowl of ice cream or some other tasty treat. You remember, however, that virtually every time you allow the child to eat too much sugar he or she gets crabby and irritable. You decide that it's better to let the child cry and complain for a while now (and get over it) so that he or she will be less grumpy later. Again, you are deferring your gratification for a short while because the payoff is worth the trade-off.

There are many other times when deferring gratification may be a good idea. You might, for example, really want to watch a certain television program, but your spouse may want or need to talk to you. Despite being disappointed about missing your favorite show, you might be wise to turn off the set and give your spouse your undivided attention. You give up a little something now for a much happier spouse later. Your relationship is enhanced and your life is less stressful as a result.

One of my own favorite ways to defer gratification occurs when the kitchen is a mess in the late evening and both Kris and I are exhausted, ready for sleep. Almost always, I force myself to stay awake long enough to clean the kitchen (deferring sleep) so that in the morning we wake up to a clean house. Both of us find that there is something peaceful about waking up and not having to start the day off with a messy kitchen. It makes the beginning of our day a little easier.

I think you'll discover that if you consider deferring gratification a little more often, it will be far easier to avoid sweating the small stuff at home.

99.

REMEMBER, THIS TOO SHALL PASS

A nugget of ancient wisdom that has served me well is the saying "This too shall pass." It has assisted me in overcoming both the day-to-day annoyances that each of us must face and some very difficult times in my life.

Think about it. Everything comes and then it goes. Problems develop and they disappear. One day we're on vacation, the next we're back to work. We get a cold or flu, and it goes away. We develop a minor injury, and in most cases it eventually heals. We anticipate an event, and the next thing you know it's over. We look forward to the Super Bowl, and the day after we're anticipating the next season.

There is enormous freedom in remembering this wisdom. In fact, it can be the foundation of a very peaceful life. It serves as an important reminder that everything has a season, a time, and a place. It gives us perspective during hard times, a frame of reference that nothing lasts forever. It gives us hope and confidence that we will get through this—it will pass; it always does.

It's tempting, for example, when you have very young children to think "I'll *never* get a good night's sleep again." Without the perspective that "this too shall pass," it's easy to get overwhelmed, even hopeless, during these difficult times. Every sleepless night seems as though it will last forever. Your mind is filled with fear. You feel hopeless, trapped, overwhelmed.

But, inevitably, as with everything, the phase passes. Then you're on to a new set of challenges—the "terrible twos," for example. The same dynamic is true with all of life's challenges. You're going through a crisis and feel you'll never get past it, but somehow you find a way. You have a big fight with your spouse and swear you'll never forgive him or her, but eventually you find it in your heart to love him or her again. You're in the midst of a particularly busy time at work and you feel you can't take it much longer, and then your schedule gets back to normal. Time and time again, we struggle and move on.

As we look back on our lives, it's easy to see that all things come and go: winter, spring, summer, and fall; joy, sorrow, praise, and blame; hardship, ease, rest, and exhaustion; accomplishments, mess-ups, and all the rest. Genuine freedom and happiness come when we can see this dynamic, not only in retrospect but while we're going through something difficult. This way, we can keep our perspective right in the midst of the chaos. When you remember that all things come and go, it allows you to keep your perspective, an open heart, and even a sense of humor during all the phases of your life.

I encourage you to remind yourself of this bit of wisdom whenever you feel annoyed, stressed, or bothered, as well as when you are going through something terribly difficult. Life is very short. Our children are little; they grow up. We are young; we grow old. We will get through it all. The best and most effective way to maintain a grateful spirit and keep yourself from being overwhelmed is to remember that all things—even the hard things—will pass.

100.

TREAT YOUR FAMILY MEMBERS AS IF THIS WERE THE LAST TIME YOU WERE GOING TO SEE THEM

It's always difficult to know how to end a book. In *Don't Sweat the Small Stuff*, I concluded by suggesting that you live as if today were your last day on earth—because it might be; you never really know. I decided to bring this book to its conclusion by making a similar suggestion, only this time geared toward your family. In this strategy, I suggest that you treat your family members (and those you love most) as if this were the last time you were going to see them.

How often do we run out the door without saying good-bye—or say something less than kind or something critical under our breath as a parting shot as we go our separate ways? How often do we take for granted those we love and count on the most, assuming we will *always* be together? Most of us seem to operate under the assumption that we can always be kind later, that there's always tomorrow. But is that a wise way to live?

A few years ago, my grandmother Emily passed away. I remember visiting her, knowing that each visit might very well be the last time I ever saw her. Each visit counted and was treated as special. Each good-bye was filled with genuine love, appreciation, and reflection. Looking back, it was a particularly loving time because each moment was precious.

Our daily lives can be this precious. A powerful exercise to practice on a regular basis is to imagine that this is your final good-bye. Imagine that, for one reason or another, you won't see your family member ever again after this meeting. If this were true (and it's always a possibility), would you think and act in the same way? Would you remind your parent, child, sibling, spouse, or other loved one of yet another shortcoming, flaw, or imperfection in his or her behavior or personality? Would your last words be complaints or pessimistic comments that suggest that you wish your life were different than it is?

Probably not.

Perhaps, if you thought there was always the possibility that this were the last time you were going to see someone you love, you'd take an extra minute to give a loving hug and say good-bye. Or maybe you'd say something kind and gentle, an affirmation of your love, instead of your business-as-usual "See you later." If you thought this were the last time you were going to see your teenager, sister, parent, in-law, or spouse, you might treat that person differently, with more kindness, and more compassionately. Rather than rushing away, you'd probably smile and tell the person how much you care. Your heart would be open.

I make this suggestion not to create a fearful environment but to encourage you to remember how precious your family is and how much you'd miss them if they (or you) weren't around to share your life with. The implementation of this strategy into my life has added additional perspective to what's most important. I believe it can help you to become more patient and loving—and perhaps most of all, to remember to not sweat the small stuff with your family.